Fort Harrison

AND THE Battle of

Chaffin's Farm

FORT HARRISON
AND THE BATTLE OF
CHAFFIN'S FARM

To Surprise and Capture Richmond

DOUGLAS CRENSHAW

THE
History
PRESS

Published by The History Press
Charleston, SC 29403
www.historypress.net

First published 2013

Manufactured in the United States

ISBN 978.1.60949.581.7

Library of Congress CIP data applied for.

Contents

Acknowledgements

I would like to take a moment to thank the people who have helped with this book. Bob Krick, chief historian for the Richmond National Battlefield Park (RNBP), has been very gracious. He has listened to my questions, assisted in finding materials, patiently read my work and offered invaluable suggestions. Any errors contained in this work are mine alone. Bob and others at the Richmond Park have assembled an amazing library of primary and secondary materials related to the Richmond battlefields, and they also have an excellent collection of photographs. Bob has been of great assistance in allowing me access to all of this, which has been essential to this book. He could not have been more generous. RNBP historians Bert Dunkerly and Mike Gorman also provided materials and offered suggestions in the preparation of this manuscript. Mike was particularly generous with his time in helping to research and study photographs and maps and in walking the battlefield with me to better understand the terrain. Thanks also to RNBP historian Ashley Luskey, who suggested the topic to me.

Bill Dunlap was very generous in allowing me to use a print of Gilbert Gaul's *Storming the Ramparts*, a striking work, and thanks to Vernon Wickstrom for his kind permission to use the image of Theodore Blakely, whose story I found to be most compelling. Alyson Rhodes-Murphy and Pam Greene of Henrico County were very generous with their time in collecting images for this work. Clifton Hyatt of the U.S. Army Heritage and Education Center, U.S. Army Military History Institute was very responsive and helpful in my search for images.

Hal Jespersen prepared the maps. As is evident, he is very talented, and his extreme patience and suggestions were invaluable. Banks Smither, my editor at The History Press, has been exceedingly helpful and patient. He has been instrumental in getting this, my first work, into print.

Finally, thanks to my wife, Judy, who suffered through the recounting of endless stories about the battles, allowed me time to work on the project and encouraged the whole undertaking.

A Note on Sources

Although a wide array of primary and secondary material was researched in the preparation of this book, a few works stand out as recommended reading for anyone who is seeking to study the topic further.

Richard J. Sommers's *Richmond Redeemed: The Siege at Petersburg* is an outstanding piece of scholarship. Dr. Sommers provides great detail, not only about the actions north of the river, but also those in the Petersburg front in the fall of 1864. The depth of his research is amazing, and it shines through in the rich detail of his text. It is a remarkable battlefield study. Any serious student of this period must consult Dr. Sommers's work.

Dr. Louis Manarin's *Henrico County Field of Honor* is a beautiful and detailed two-volume study of the Civil War experience of Henrico County, Virginia. Deeply researched, it contains good maps and many paintings, pictures and illustrations. It is a very enjoyable read. The first volume covers through 1862, and the larger second volume addresses the remainder of the war. An interesting postlude discusses what became of the battlefields in the century and a half following the war. The two-book set is available through the County of Henrico Department of Parks and Recreation, and the Richmond National Battlefield Park often carries them in its Tredegar Bookstore.

For a study of the Battle of New Market Heights, James S. Price's *The Battle of New Market Heights: Freedom Will Be Theirs by the Sword* is required reading. Jimmy studies the "right flank" of Ben Butler's attack on September 29, and he covers the involvement of the United States Colored Troops (USCTs) with depth and respect. I highly recommend it.

Prologue

Fort Harrison is not a famous name like Gettysburg, Antietam or Vicksburg. It's not even one of the better-known sites in the Richmond National Battlefield Park system. Many more visitors travel to Cold Harbor, Gaines' Mill and Malvern Hill. This is unfortunate because the actions at Chaffin's Farm on September 29 and 30, 1864, were critically important. The Union came closer to capturing Richmond than at any other time during the war, until that city surrendered in April 1865. Thousands of lives potentially could have been saved had the Federal attack been completely successful.

For many of the men who fought at Chaffin's Farm, these would be the most important and most terrifying days of their lives. Indeed, many of these brave men—husbands, fathers and sons—perished fighting on these fields. Others suffered terrible and often life-changing wounds. African American soldiers not only faced the possibility of death in combat, but if captured, they were also presented with the real threat of being sent into slavery. We do well to pause on what happened here, to think of the brave men who fought and the desperate action that took place. In his study of an American army fighting in a later war, Rick Atkinson said it well: "The author's task is to authenticate: to warrant that history and memory give integrity to the story, to aver that all of this really happened. But the final few steps must be the reader's. For among mortal powers, only imagination can bring back the dead."[1]

Chapter 1

The Summer of '64

It was May 1864, the fourth summer of the war. Over the previous three years, President Lincoln had tried a succession of commanders to lead the Army of the Potomac, but none seemed to be able to bring Robert E. Lee and his vaunted Army of Northern Virginia to bay. Frustrated by the lack of initiative by his army since its victory at Gettysburg, Lincoln summoned Ulysses S. Grant from the west to be the commander of all Union armies. Grant had been the hero of Forts Henry and Donelson, Shiloh and Vicksburg and seemed to have the fighting spirit and determination that had been lacking in the top level of the Army of the Potomac. There was no doubt that the rank and file of that army possessed all the courage and will to fight that anyone could ask for, as they had proven time and time again. They just needed leadership, and Lincoln was betting it all on Grant. There would be a presidential election in 1864. With the mounting losses of the past three years, and nothing to show for it in the eastern theater, time could well be running out.

Grant saw things clearly. The North had the advantages in men, production and transportation, and he was determined to use those advantages in a way that had not been effectively done before. Lincoln and Grant realized that the goal should be the defeat of the two large Confederate armies, one under Joseph Johnston in the West and the Army of Northern Virginia under Lee. If these two armies were destroyed, the South would no longer be able to carry on with significant resistance. The focus of all the Union forces would be to bring these two armies out and destroy them. Grant would "work

Ulysses S. Grant. *LOC.*

Robert E. Lee. *LOC.*

all parts of the Army together, and somewhat towards a common centre."[2]

In the West, the job was assigned to William T. Sherman, and in the East, three forces would move against Lee. George Meade would remain in command of the Army of the Potomac, whose objective was to get Lee's army out in the open and destroy it. Franz Sigel would lead an army through the Shenandoah Valley, and Benjamin Butler would bring his Army of the James up from Norfolk and land at Bermuda Hundred, between Richmond and Petersburg. Butler's movement would threaten both cities and keep vital reinforcements from joining Lee. Grant would travel with the Army of the Potomac. His plan was for all of the armies to move in early May.

For his part, Lee generally had to assume the defensive. The Army of Northern Virginia was not the same fighting force it had been only a year before. Irreplaceable casualties, the loss of many key leaders, including Stonewall Jackson and soon James Longstreet, and a tenuous supply situation had taken much of the punch out of it. However, Lee did not plan to sit idly by and let Grant take and keep the initiative. He would wait for an opportunity and strike a blow. Should Grant be allowed the upper hand, Lee knew that his opponent's advantage in numbers, combined with the availability of a constant stream of Northern troops and supplies, would lead to only one result, that of pure arithmetic. No, Lee must try to grab the initiative as early as possible.[3]

On May 4, the Army of the Potomac moved south. Before it could reach open ground, the Union army had to travel through a wooded area thick with underbrush locally known as "the Wilderness." While Lee faced the Federal army of about 120,000 with his force of some 65,000 men,[4] he was used to such long odds, and his army's morale was high. He determined that he could best neutralize the Federal advantages in men and artillery by drawing them into a fight in the thickets of the Wilderness. As soon as the Union forces crossed the Rapidan, Lee moved two of his corps into the Wilderness, threatening the Union army, while he waited for his third corps to arrive. The Federals attacked, and the ensuing battle lasted for two days. It appeared that the Confederates were on the brink of a stunning victory when General Longstreet was wounded by his own men as he led a charge that threatened to crush the Union flank. Ironically, it had been almost a year to the day and in proximity that Stonewall Jackson had been shot by his men while leading a brilliant flanking charge at Chancellorsville. Losses for both sides were severe. The Union lost approximately 17,000 men, or 14 percent of its entire force, and the Confederates lost 11,000.[5] The key difference was that the Lee could no longer afford such losses.

The Wilderness. *LOC.*

As their army left the field, it must have seemed like a repeat of the same old story to the Federal troops. Face Robert E. Lee, lose and then retreat. This time, however, things would be different. Grant had no intention of retreating; he was going to keep after Lee. As the Federals left the battlefield and reached the north–south road, Grant did something his predecessors had not: he turned south. Grant meant to keep fighting, and he directed his troops to the crossroads at Spotsylvania Court House. If they could beat Lee to that place, they would be between the Confederates and Richmond, and the Southerners would be forced to fight out in the open. Grant would have another opportunity to destroy Lee.

The Confederates won the race to the Court House by the narrowest of margins, and the ensuing battle witnessed some of the most savage fighting ever seen on the North American continent. Fighting hand to hand and with desperate intensity, casualties were enormous. Grant could not drive Lee away, but on May 11, he wrote to General Halleck, the army chief of staff, "I am satisfied the enemy are very shaky, and are only kept up to the mark by the greatest exertions on the part of their officers, and by keeping them intrenched [*sic*] in every position they take. [I] propose to fight it out on this line if it takes all summer."[6] An authority on the 1864 Overland Campaign, Gordon Rhea

Spotsylvania. *LOC.*

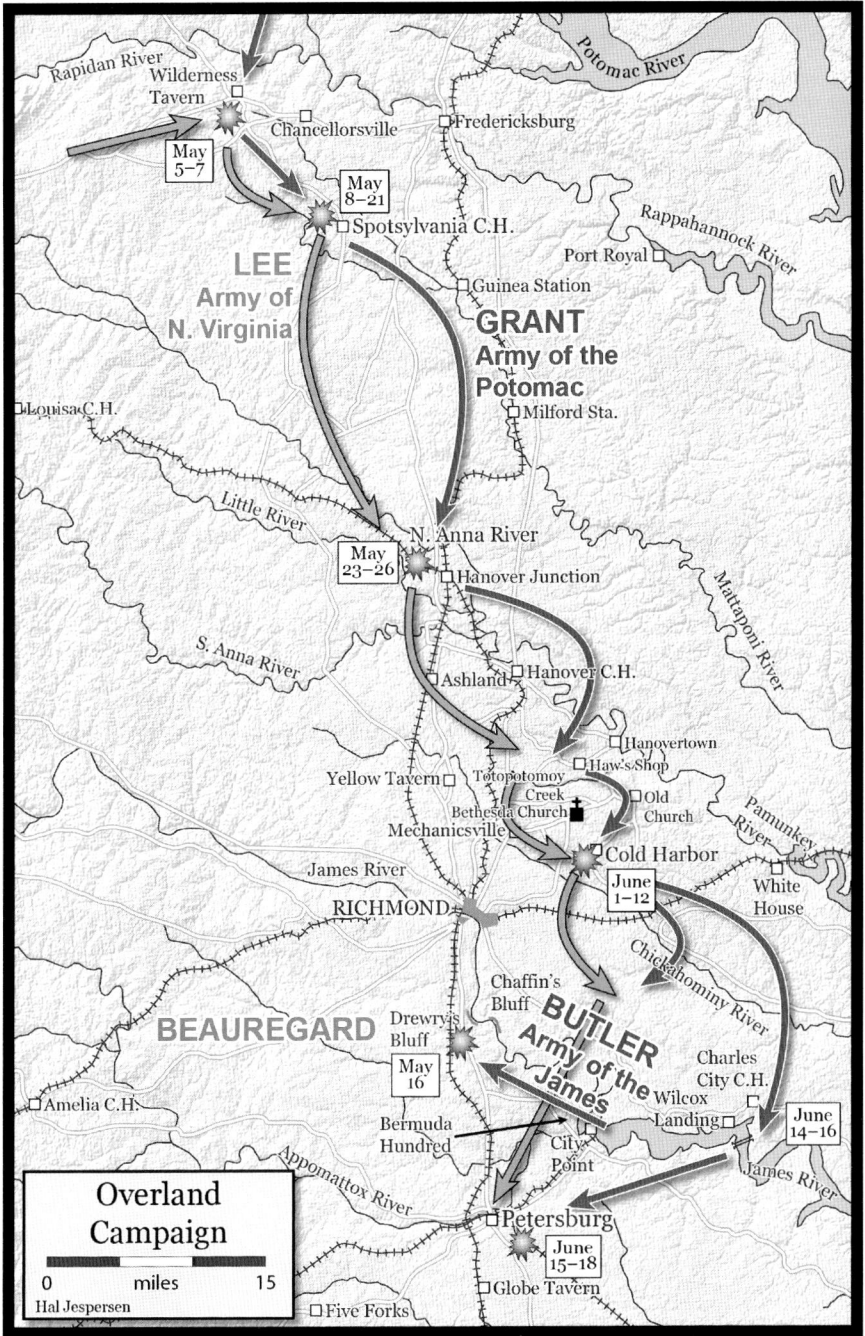

Map of the Virginia Theater. *Hal Jespersen.*

commented that Grant's initiative and persistence were taking a toll on Lee's army and that "Lincoln finally had a general who shared his resolution to batter the Army of Northern Virginia steadfastly until it collapsed."[7]

Following the carnage at Spotsylvania, Grant once again drove south around Lee's right flank. Again Lee won the race, this time to the banks of the North Anna River. Here the effect of the leadership losses in the Confederate high command was clearly evident. Lee set a trap for the Federals. Unfortunately for the Southern army, Lee became ill, and he didn't have a Jackson or Longstreet to spring the trap. Lee had missed one of his best chances and one of his last. The Federals escaped and then continued their pattern of moving around Lee's right flank and heading south. Once again, Lee got ahead of them, this time heading them off at Totopotomoy Creek, on the outskirts of Richmond. There was fighting on that creek, at nearby Bethesda Church, and on June 1, the Federals launched an attack at the crossroads at Cold Harbor, which nearly succeeded but suffered for lack of supporting troops. Nearly two years had passed since the two armies clashed on almost exactly the same ground, at the Battle of Gaines' Mill.

On hearing word of the near success at Cold Harbor, Grant determined to launch a major assault there the next day, but he could not get all of his troops in position in time to attack on June 2. The assault was postponed until June 3, but that proved to be a day too late. Lee took advantage of the time and got his troops in position and entrenched in strength. When the Federals did attack, they had little chance, and the result was slaughter. Grant later lamented, "I have always regretted that the last assault at Cold Harbor was ever made. At Cold Harbor, no advantage whatever was gained for the heavy loss we sustained."[8]

It had been a little more than a month since Grant opened his campaign. He had failed to bring Lee out into the open and destroy him. Lee had fought a masterful game of checking the Federals' every move and entrenching to even the odds. However, he was short on men, food and now even room to maneuver. What had this cost the two armies? The Confederates, who had begun the campaign with some 65,000 men, had lost about 33,000, or close to 50 percent of their nearly irreplaceable manpower. Grant started out with 120,000 and lost between 52,000 and 55,000. While both totals were staggering, Grant's percentage was lower, and he could replace his losses.[9] He was winning the war of attrition, but would the Northern populace continue to tolerate it?

In the Shenandoah Valley, Jubal Early chased off his Federal opponents and drove to the very gates of Washington. To ease Lincoln's anxiety over the threat to the capital, Grant sent the Sixth Corps north to Washington to

Cold Harbor Tavern. *LOC.*

confront Early. In August, he also sent Phil Sheridan to lead a newly organized army group, and Sheridan drove Early back down into Virginia, defeating him at Winchester and at Fisher's Hill. The Confederacy's vital hold on its breadbasket in the valley was slipping away. Despite this good news, Lincoln still worried, "I am a little afraid lest Lee sends re-enforcements to Early, and thus enables him to turn upon Sheridan."[10] The threat to Washington, real or imagined, was never far from the president's mind.

After the failed June 3 assault at Cold Harbor, Grant considered his next move. On June 5, he wrote to the army's chief of staff, General Halleck:

> *My idea from the start has been to beat Lee's army if possible north of Richmond; then after destroying his lines of communication on the north side of the James River to transfer the army to the south side and besiege Richmond, or follow him south if he should retreat. I now find, after thirty days of trial, the enemy deems it of first importance to run no risks with the army they now have. They act purely on the defensive behind breastworks, or feebly in the offensive immediately in front of them, and where in the case of repulse they can instantly retire behind them. Without a greater sacrifice of human life than I am willing to make all cannot be accomplished that I had designed outside the city.*[11]

Jubal
Early.
LOC.

Grant's plan was to have the Army of the Potomac cross the James River and, in combination with the army in the valley, cut off all sources of supply to the Confederate army and to Richmond. On June 12, he began his move and crossed the James on June 14 and 15. On the fifteenth, two Federal corps approached the thinly manned defenses at Petersburg. William F. "Baldy" Smith's Eighteenth Corps led the first attacks but moved cautiously toward the enemy's earthworks. At Spotsylvania, North Anna and particularly at Cold Harbor, the men had seen the damage that could be inflicted by a firmly entrenched opponent. For the next two days, a tremendous opportunity was missed, as the Federals greatly outnumbered their Confederate counterparts but failed to take advantage of their numbers. Petersburg had been theirs for the taking. Lee, quickly realizing that Grant had stolen a march on him, rushed his forces to the Petersburg area. Soon the opposing forces would be locked in a deadly, static situation, from south of Petersburg to the eastern approaches to Richmond. This would last until the following April.

In July, Grant attempted to break the stalemate. On the twenty-sixth, Hancock's corps and Sheridan's cavalry were sent to the north side of the James in an attempt to draw some of Lee's troops away from the trenches at Petersburg. At night on the twenty-ninth, the Federal forces returned to the south side of the river, and on July 30, the Union forces exploded a mine under Confederate earthworks, with the aim of breaking the line and driving on to Petersburg. A great opportunity was wasted. The affair was badly mismanaged, and troops were needlessly sacrificed in the fiasco known as the Battle of the Crater. Grant wrote to Halleck, "It was the saddest affair I have witnessed in the war. Such opportunity for carrying fortifications I have never seen and do not expect again to have."[12]

In August, Grant again attempted to attack both ends of Lee's line. While not successful, it did have the effect of forcing Lee to further extend his lines, which now reached for thirty-five miles.[13] Confederate forces were severely strained. On August 22, Lee wrote to the secretary of war that the enemy's "purpose now is to compel us to evacuate it by cutting off our supplies."[14] He followed the next day by saying, "Without some increase of strength, I cannot see how we are to escape the natural military consequences of the enemy's numerical superiority."[15]

Sherman took Atlanta, Sheridan advanced down the Shenandoah Valley and Grant had pushed Lee back to the fortifications around Petersburg. What of the other part of the Federal offensive, that of Benjamin Butler and his Army of the James? Prior to the beginning of the 1864 campaign, he and Grant had met and planned that Butler would take the Tenth and Eighteenth Corps, consisting of approximately thirty thousand men, up the James River and land on Bermuda Hundred, a small peninsula that lay between the James and Appomattox Rivers. Butler was to secure a base of operations, one that could be protected against a Confederate attack. A major Rebel railroad was within a few miles, and Petersburg and Richmond were not far beyond. If Butler moved swiftly, he could cut the railroad, a vital supply link to the Southern states, and then threaten Petersburg and Richmond. He would heavily outnumber any available Confederate troops, and this would force Lee to send reinforcements that he desperately needed to hold off the Army of the Potomac.[16] The Southern army could be stretched to the breaking point.

Facing Butler's host was a small Confederate force, plus local militia. Their commander, P.G.T. Beauregard, had not yet arrived. Butler seemed more intent on building a secure base than on seizing the opportunity before him. He launched a half-hearted attack on May 6, when a full-scale assault might have won the day. During this battle at Port Walthall Junction, the Union used only nineteen regiments out of Butler's two corps, and of those, only six regiments were engaged. With approximately 2,600 men on hand, the Confederates had averted a near disaster. Butler was not on the scene; he was back at his base, ensuring its safety against perceived threats from the enemy.[17] On May 9, Federal forces advanced on Drewry's Bluff, the site of Union frustration in 1862. They pierced the outer works but did not advance any farther. Soon Beauregard and more Confederate reinforcements arrived, and on May 16, they drove the Federals back. The little peninsula proved to be an excellent position from which the Southerners could block Butler's army. There Butler's force remained, "in a position of great security, was as completely shut off from further operations against Richmond as if it had been in a bottle strongly corked."[18] They were so ineffective that Grant took the Eighteenth Corps and sent it to Cold Harbor, where it participated in the attack of June 3. Another tremendous Union opportunity had been squandered.

Chapter 2

A Plan Develops

Benjamin Butler was a controversial but interesting character. A successful and politically connected lawyer from Massachusetts, he parlayed his political connections to become a brigadier general in the Massachusetts infantry. In the early stages of the war, it was not certain whether Maryland would remain in the Union, and Butler and his troops secured Baltimore in April 1861, arresting pro-Confederate officials. The latter action alarmed Lincoln, but realizing the strength of Butler's political connections, he assigned him to an out-of-the-way post at Fort Monroe, Virginia, in 1861. In a move to attract political favor, Lincoln had Butler promoted to major general in May 1861.[19] Butler was defeated in an action at Big Bethel in June of that year, but in August, he was successful in taking two Confederate coastal forts in North Carolina.

During his stay at Fort Monroe, Butler came up with a unique solution to the growing number of slaves who ran away from their masters and sought refuge with the Union army. Owners would turn up to claim their property, which was legal under the Fugitive Slave Act of 1850. Butler struggled with what to do with the runaways. Early in the war, this was a difficult question. On July 30, he wrote to Secretary of War Simon Cameron:

> *Indeed it was a most distressing sight to see these poor creatures, who had trusted to the protection of the arms of the United States, and who aided the troops of the United States in their enterprise, to be thus obliged to flee from their homes, and the homes of their masters, who had deserted*

Benjamin Butler. *LOC.*

them, and become fugitives from fear of the return of the rebel soldiery, who had threatened to shoot the men who had wrought for us, and to carry off the women who had served us to a worse than Egyptian bondage…who are to be considered fugitive whose master runs away and leaves him? Is it forbidden to the troops to aid or harbor within their lines the negro [sic] children who are found therein, or is the soldier, when his march has destroyed their means of subsistence, to allow them to starve because he has driven off the rebel masters?[20]

Butler invented a clever scheme; he was stationed in Virginia, which had removed itself from the Union. As the Fugitive Slave Act was only applicable in the United States, he declared the slaves to be "contraband of war."[21] This served two purposes: it gave the slaves desperately needed refuge, and it also weakened the Southern war effort by reducing available labor needed to run the farms.

After the fall of New Orleans, Butler was placed in command of the Union occupation of that city, and it was a most controversial tenure. In an effort to maintain order, he declared martial law and demanded that the citizens take a loyalty oath to the Union. One of the most notorious incidents involved resident William Mumford, who was arrested for desecrating a Union flag. Butler had Mumford hanged, ignoring the pleadings of his wife, who would be left to take care of their children. Harsh as his decision was, Butler demonstrated compassion years later when he provided financial assistance to Mumford's wife and secured a position for her in the internal revenue office.[22]

On May 15, 1862, Butler issued his infamous Order #28, which stated that any woman who insulted a Union officer would be "held liable to be treated as a woman of the town plying her avocation."[23] From that time on, Butler's name was notorious in the South, and he became known as the "Beast." While he did maintain order in the captured city and showed compassion to those in need, his name was frequently associated with rumors of corruption. Lincoln ultimately removed Butler but, cognizant of the support Butler had from the Democratic Party, sent him back to Fort Monroe, where he was given command of the corps that composed the Army of the James.[21]

Whatever his shortcomings as a military commander, Butler did possess some abilities. He developed an effective spy network that consisted of Confederate deserters, escaped slaves and Union loyalists. One of the most famous (or infamous, to most of those who lived in Richmond) was Elizabeth Van Lew. Her family owned a farm on the Richmond–Henrico County line, and she used it as one of the points through which she could pass information to Butler and later to Grant. Van Lew employed ingenious methods: "Information was delivered by servants carrying baskets of eggs. One of the eggs in each basket was hollow and contained her notes, which had been torn into small pieces. In addition, messages were carried in the soles of servants' shoes. She devised her own code consisting of numbers and letters."[25] Other local residents, like Alfred R. Buffin, a peaceful man, were known to help escaped slaves and Confederate deserters.[26] Many of these came with useful information.

As September rolled on, Grant pondered his next move; he decided to make another of his two-pronged attacks. This time he would send six thousand to ten thousand men to strike at Cape Fear, North Carolina, in an attempt to cut off the blockade-runners that were using the port of Wilmington. With his main force, south of Petersburg, he would strike west and try to cut the South Side railroad leading to Petersburg. This would leave the railroad that ran southwest to Danville as the only major supply line remaining to Richmond. October 5 was set as the date for his assault.[27]

The situation north of the James was quiet in early September. After the Union army's forays of late July and mid-August, there was only a modest-sized force left north of the river.[28] Facing them was a massive series of earthwork defenses that the Confederates had been erecting since 1862. As with any major city, roads radiated into Richmond, much like the spokes on a wheel. From the northeast to the southeast, a network of roads provided excellent avenues of approach for an invading force coming from the east. The major roads included Mechanicsville Turnpike and, moving clockwise, Nine Mile Road, Williamsburg Road, Charles City Road, Darbytown Road, New Market Road (partially fed by Varina Road) and Osborne Turnpike.

Defending all of these approaches was an enormous challenge. Adding to this was the increasingly limited manpower the Confederacy had to draw upon.

In an effort to meet potential threats, the defenders had constructed a large and complicated series of works. Immediately surrounding the capital was a series of star-shaped forts containing heavy artillery. Farther out, five miles from the city, was a line of works known as the Intermediate Defenses that ran from the James River all the way north to Mechanicsville Turnpike, then to Brook Road and to Westham Turnpike. Another series of entrenchments, the Outer Line, ran from Fort Harrison and surrounded the city. An additional line ran out to New Market Heights. In appearance, the defenses were daunting.[29]

Chaffin's Bluff was on the extreme southeastern end of the defenses. Combined with the Confederate works across the James River at Drewry's Bluff, the river defenses there were a formidable obstacle to any Federal naval units attempting to reach Richmond by water. The bluff was situated on part of the farm of Susan Chaffin, which, owing to its significant location, had been converted into a Confederate armed camp. The farm was strategically located between the Osborne Turnpike to the west and Varina Road to the east. Forts Maury and Hoke controlled the approach to Richmond via the Osborne Turnpike. Fort Maury sat on a significant rise, and Fort Hoke was a short distance to the northeast. Their combined fire would interdict any advance in that direction. Moving inland, the strongest set of Confederate works was built on a dominating hill, the rise steep from the west, south and east. It commanded the area in reach of its artillery. That fortification would become known as Fort Harrison. To the north and slightly west was Fort Gilmer, which could interdict any approaches by the Varina or New Market Roads. Slightly farther to the east, the Confederates had constructed a line to New Market Heights, which dominated the New Market Road approach. To a Federal army that had painful experience in attacking an entrenched enemy, these works were imposing indeed and had to be taken very seriously.

As intimidating as the Confederate entrenchments appeared, reports were coming in from spies and deserters of Confederate strength, or the lack of it, north of the river. Several deserters laid out the Confederate troop placements from New Market Heights to "Aiken's" on the river. Many of the defenders were stationed on the Confederate right, near the river. On the left was the Texas Brigade, now woefully under strength. It was a mere shadow of the formidable brigade of the war's earlier days, averaging only 150 men in each regiment.[30] There were roughly 4,400 men in gray between the James River and New Market Heights, plus another 1,500 from the Intermediate defenses who could be brought up. Added to this were some 2,700 local reserves and militia that could respond from Richmond.[31] While Butler's estimate of Confederate strength was low, approximately 3,000 men, the quality of these troops was suspect. As mentioned, there were remnants of the Texas Brigade, legendary for its bravery during the war. Bushrod Johnson's once-solid Tennessee Brigade was on hand, but it had been spent by years of heavy fighting. Added to these were remnants of Benning's Georgia Brigade, some cavalry, heavy artillerists from the fortifications and inexperienced local militia and

Bushrod Johnson. *LOC.*

the "City Battalion," who would be of dubious worth when facing veterans of the Army of the James.[32]

Estimates of actual Confederate strength vary. In his biography of General Richard S. Ewell, Donald Pfanz said that their numbers were close to 8,600. General Porter Alexander later estimated that Southerners had about 6,000 men north of the James.[33] Confederate returns on September 20 showed that Ewell had 5,985 present north of the river,[34] and added to this were Gregg's troops in the New Market Heights area. In any case, Butler could easily outnumber them with his two corps and cavalry, numbering close to 26,600 men.[35]

Although his left flank north of the river was very weak, Lee had little choice. The strongest of the Union forces, the Army of the Potomac, faced him outside Petersburg. Grant was an aggressive commander who could not be ignored. Lee had the solid series of earthworks protecting the capital, which could help to even the odds. He also had four bridges over the river and could shuttle troops quickly to any threatened sector. He had to play the odds and keep an eye on Grant.

Several key factors compounded the challenges to the Confederates stationed north of the river. The top officers charged with Richmond's eastern defenses were of dubious quality. Braxton Bragg, discredited for his leadership in the West, had been brought to Richmond as President Davis's special advisor. John C. Pemberton, the general Grant had defeated at Vicksburg, was in charge of the artillery. Of perhaps the greatest concern was Richard S. Ewell. Once a solid and promising commander under Stonewall Jackson, Ewell had lost a leg at Second Manassas. Upon his return to the army, he was given command of the Second Corps. His performances at Gettysburg, the Wilderness and Spotsylvania Court House had not impressed Lee, who had him reassigned to Richmond.[36] How would he perform if pressed?

Another challenge was that Gregg's troops reported to the Army of Northern Virginia. Ewell was in charge of the Richmond defenses but did not technically have command over Gregg.[37] A split command could be a dangerous liability in a combat situation. Realizing this, Lee attempted to remedy this situation on September 28[38] by ordering the commander of the First Corps, General Richard Anderson, to assume command north of the James. However, it was too late; by the time Anderson arrived at Chaffin's Bluff, the battle would already be seven hours old.[39] With the leadership divided and the strongest forces separated on the left and right, the Confederates were the most vulnerable in the center, at Fort Harrison, the very key to their position. An attack there would jeopardize the entire defensive line and just might open the door to Richmond. If the Confederates didn't face enough challenges, their reserves consisted of men from the local defense forces and the 1,500 stationed in the Intermediate Defenses. How would these unproven men react to battle?

Armed with information about the defenders, Butler met with Grant and proposed an attack north of the James. Impressed with Butler's scheme, Grant cancelled his Cape Fear plans and decided instead to launch two simultaneous efforts, with Meade capturing the Southside Railroad below Petersburg and Butler driving at the Confederate capital. While he may not have been as optimistic about the capture of Richmond as was Butler,[10] Grant knew that such a move would strain Lee's already thin forces. If Lee shifted troops north to meet Butler's offensive, Meade and the Army of the Potomac could take the railroad. If Lee didn't respond, which was unlikely, then perhaps Butler's plan just might succeed. In any case, Grant changed his target from Cape Fear to north of the James. Upon hearing that the Confederates might be preparing to evacuate Petersburg,[11] he moved the attack to September 29.

Grant's plan called for Butler to take his two corps and cross the James and attack the fortifications east of Richmond, while Meade would take twenty-five thousand men and attack toward the railroad below Petersburg. Half of Grant's entire army would participate in the action. On September 27, he informed Meade of the dual-pronged offensive and instructed him to be ready to move at 4:00 a.m. on the twenty-ninth, with four days' cooked rations in the men's haversacks and sixty rounds of ammunition. He left the details to Meade but said, "I want every effort used to convince the enemy that the South Side road and Petersburg are the objects of our efforts…if the road is reached, or a position commanding it, it should be held against all hazards."[42]

Grant wrote to Butler the same day:

> *The movement should be commenced at night, and so as to get a considerable force north of the James River, ready to assault the enemy's lines above Deep Bottom, and from Aiken's house or other point above Deep Bottom, the two assaulting columns will be in easy supporting distance of each other, as soon as the enemy's line is broken at the dawn of the day…the object of this move is to surprise and capture Richmond, if possible. This cannot be done if time is given the enemy to move forces to the north side of the river. Success will depend on prompt movement at the start. Should the outer line be broken, the troops will push for Richmond with all promptness, following roads as near the river as possible…as the success of the enterprise depends entirely on celerity, the troops will go light. They will take only a single blanket rolled and carried over the shoulder, three days' rations in haversacks and sixty rounds of ammunition in box and on the person. No wagons will be taken. They will be supplied, however, with six days' rations, half forage for the same time, and forty rounds of extra ammunition for men, to follow if they should be required. No wagons will cross the James River till ordered by you…if the enemy resists you by sufficient force to prevent your advance, it is confidently expected that General Meade can gain a decisive advantage on his end of the line. The prize sought is either Richmond or Petersburg, or a position which will secure the fall of the latter.*[43]

The commanders for Butler's wing of the attack would be Edward Ord, leading the Eighteenth Corps in place of Baldy Smith, and David Birney commanding the Tenth Corps. Ord was an old army regular but, due to illness and wounds, had limited combat experience, having fought only two battles in the war. Bold leadership combined with personal heroism was

Ord's concept of the ideal traits for a battlefield commander. This would be his great opportunity. The other corps commander, David Birney, was a lawyer by profession. Unlike Ord, however, he had experience and had been handpicked by Grant to lead the Tenth Corps. August Kautz would lead the cavalry, but he had not proven effective in command thus far.[44]

Butler's orders of September 28 explained the purpose of the attack. They stated that the bridge the Eighteenth Corps was to take across the James was to be in place by midnight of the twenty-eighth. Ord was to cross on this bridge, taking the First and Second Divisions. His Third Division, consisting of USCTs, was to be temporarily attached to the Tenth Corps, which would cross farther east at Deep Bottom. Butler knew his force greatly outnumbered the defenders and that the enemy troops were of varying quality. He understood the fortifications and the bridges the Confederates could use to send reinforcements. Butler emphasized the need for speed and surprise, saying, "A large element of the complete success of this movement depends upon its celerity and the co-operation in point of time of the several commands in the attack." Ord was to mass his troops near Varina "during the night, silently, so as not to be observed by the enemy, and from thence just before daybreak, which is assumed to be 4:30 a.m., and that will govern in point of time, to make a sudden, sharp attack in column upon the enemy's lines nearly opposite his position on the Varina Road." He was then to move up the Varina Road and take the works at Chaffin's, if possible, but he was "expressly cautioned, however, to lose no time in attempting to envelop Chaffin's farm." He was to attack the "line of works extending across his path" in the Chaffin's Farm area and then proceed to "secure and destroy the pontoon crossing just above." After securing the bridge area, Ord was to leave sufficient force to protect his rear and then "push up toward the New Market Road" and meet up with General Birney's Tenth Corps, which by that time should have been moving up the New Market Road. They would both then proceed toward Richmond.

Ord was to destroy any other bridges by which the Confederate could bring up reinforcements. Butler thought that if Ord could accomplish this, "there can be but little doubt of the complete success of the movement." Butler continued: "The commanding general of the army will endeavor to keep himself in communication with the corps commanders, so as to afford any direction, advice, or assistance that may be in his power, and by being kept advised of the movements of the one and the other of the corps commanders, as well as the command of General Kautz, may be thus enabled to secure more perfect co-operation than would otherwise be possible."[45]

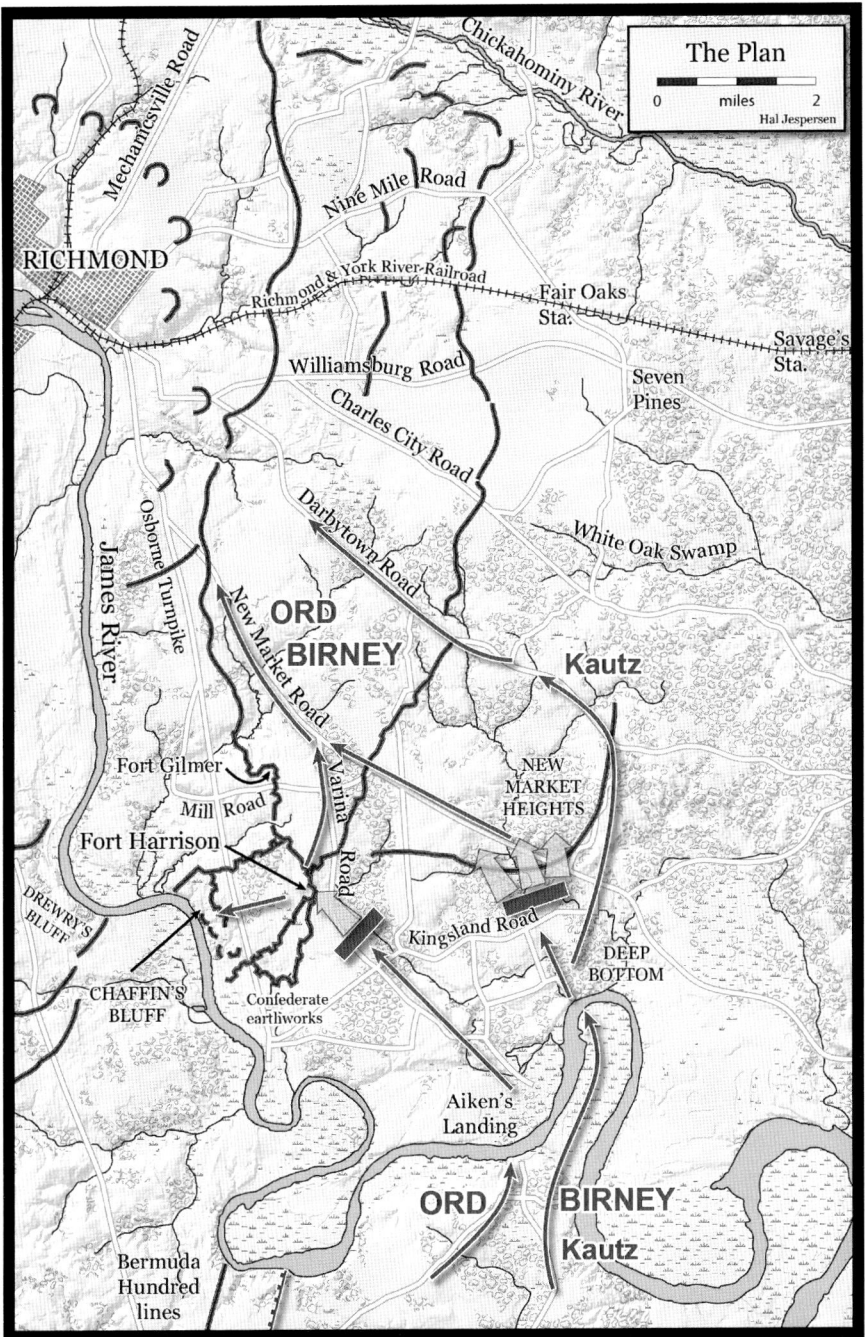

Map of the Union plan. *Hal Jespersen.*

This bridge across the James is similar to the one used by Ord's troops. *LOC.*

Butler repeated Grant's instructions about traveling light, with no wagons accompanying the troops, and stated, "As this movement will necessarily be a failure if it degenerates into an artillery duel, there is no necessity or any artillery to cross until after the attempt to carry the first line of works…the commanding general is under no substantial mistake in regard to the force to be at first encountered, and therefore there is no necessity of time spent in reconnoitering or taking special care of the flanks of moving columns." As an incentive "the commanding general will recommend for promotion to the next higher grade, the brigadier-general commanding the division, colonel commanding brigade, and so on down to all officers and soldiers of the leading division, brigade, or regiment which first enters Richmond." Butler added an additional enticement: "If Richmond is taken, he will pledge to the division, brigade or regiment first entering the city, to each officer and man, six months' extra pay."[16]

At Aiken's landing, the Federals had gathered seventy-seven pontoon boats but, to ensure surprise, had to wait until after dark to begin their work. As they crossed the river and neared the other side, the engineers discovered a muddy bank and low tide. They had to drag the remaining boats over the muck, but nonetheless they were finished, having laid a 1,320-foot bridge consisting of sixty-seven boats by 2:00 a.m. Dirt and straw were spread across the bridge to muffle any sounds.[17] The troops were in position and waiting for the appointed hour.

New York Times reporter Jacob Wisner, who had been an officer with a New York Zouave regiment earlier in the war, commented on the manner in which Butler's movement was kept quiet. "In all my experience I never before knew a plan to be kept so profoundly secret."[18]

Chapter 3

Dawn, September 29

The commander of Ord's First Division, George J. Stannard, was no stranger to combat. Born in Vermont in 1820, he had fought at First Manassas and on the Peninsula in 1862. Captured at Harpers Ferry during the Antietam Campaign, he was later exchanged and subsequently saw action at Gettysburg, where he led his Vermont troops in a flank attack against Pickett's Charge on July 3 and was wounded in the right thigh. At Cold Harbor, he was wounded in the left thigh and in his ankle, and at Petersburg he was hit in the left hand.[49] He had suffered personally and had seen too many brave young men pay the price for poor planning and execution. Chosen to lead Ord's attack at Chaffin's Farm, he had serious reservations.

Years later, Stannard told Ripley that he went to headquarters to protest but was informed, "General Grant had personally chosen his division to lead the attack." He went to see Grant, who was at Deep Bottom, and said to him, "I am told that I must lead this attack, and I have come to protest in behalf of the poor men of my division, who have led every assault of the Eighteenth Corps, from Cold Harbor until now, and are fought down to a skeleton of a division." He continued, "I have not a word to say for myself—I will freely go wherever you send me; but it is inhuman to give my men so much more than their share of these forlorn hopes." To this Grant replied, "General Stannard, we must carry Fort Harrison, and I know you will do it." Ripley commented, "Stannard, ever the consummate soldier, knew when to salute and execute, and he returned to his division to prepare his men for the next day's action."[50] Prepare he did, but the attack at Fort Harrison was to cost Stannard dearly.

Ord's Second Division was led by Charles A. Heckman, a former seminarian who had enlisted for the Mexican War. Following that war, he worked as a conductor for the Central Railroad of New Jersey. When the Civil War came, he enlisted again and took part in Burnside's expedition on the North Carolina coast in 1862. He had been promoted to colonel in '62 and to brigadier general in November of the same year.[51]

George J. Stannard. *LOC.*

It is unclear exactly how many men Ord took with him across the river. In his official report, he stated that he led 4,000 troops. Union general Andrew A. Humphreys corroborates that, as does S. Millett Thompson, a lieutenant in the Thirteenth Regiment of the New Hampshire Volunteers, as well as historian Louis Manarin. Richard Sommers has studied the question in depth and makes a convincing argument that Ord had 8,135 men.[52] Ord understood that surprise would be the key to the ultimate success of the assault, and in keeping with Butler's instructions concerning secrecy, he stated, "The movement was to be a surprise, therefore I issued no written orders, and my verbal orders were not to be communicated to the troops until after dark, when all communications should have ceased with our picket line." In an area teeming with enemy eyes and ears, "this precaution was deemed necessary to prevent the spies which abounded in our regiments from deserting and giving information of our movement to the enemy."[53]

After clearing out the Confederate skirmishers near the river, Ord's first objective was the key work on the Confederate line, the imposing fortification at Fort Harrison. Named for William E. Harrison, who laid out the defenses that were constructed by a combination of infantry and slave labor,[54] it sat on high ground and commanded a plateau running down to Varina Road. The fort was the most important position in a chain of Confederate batteries that ran along the line. They had names like Fort Maury, Fort Hoke, Fort Gilmer, Battery X and the White Battery, and others were numbered (Battery 10, Battery 11, etc.).

Edward O. Ord is seen with his family, sitting at the Confederate White House after the fall of Richmond. *LOC.*

Harrison had a dry moat and ramparts that reached up to eighteen feet high. Interior walls were reinforced with logs from slashed timber.[55] It had some field guns, including two eight-inch Columbiads, a one-hundred-pound Parrott, a forty and two thirty-two-pounders and a thirty-pounder. As Richard Sommers has so aptly stated, "The problem…was not the caliber but the condition of the guns." Many of the guns had been spiked and were thus inoperable, and others had ammunition that was too large to fit. As few as four guns may have been operable.[56] Although the fort was large enough to accommodate a sizable garrison, it was woefully undermanned, having only about two hundred men available to defend it,[57] mostly artillerists from the Goochland Artillery, militia and troops from the Seventeenth Georgia.[58] To make matters even worse, those present were armed with smoothbore muskets with only ten rounds apiece.[59]

Their smoothbores would be useless until the enemy was within one hundred yards.

In command of the Confederate position was Major Richard Cornelius Taylor, who was filling in for the absent Lieutenant Colonel John Maury.[60] Born in 1835, Taylor had attended the Virginia Military Institute, and he was a teacher and an auditor prior to the war. His brother was the noted Walter H. Taylor, the assistant adjutant general to Robert E. Lee.[61] Normally a staff officer, Taylor faced an overwhelming challenge. Behind his ramparts, he would defend against the Union host with a small garrison of varying quality. They had a few serviceable guns, and there was an alarming lack of

William E. Harrison. *RNBP.*

obstacles in the path of the attackers. Importantly, there were no abatis, timber slashings strewn to slow down an enemy advance. Slowing down an attacker provided the defenders an opportunity to get more shots off and consequently inflict more casualties. Without such defenses, the Federals would come at them across an open field. Had there been abatis and quality artillery with plenty of ammunition, the field might have proven a more defendable killing ground, but such was not the case. Taylor would fight with what he had and do his utmost to keep the back door to Richmond closed.

At the bridge, the Federal troops were waiting to cross the river. Lieutenant R.B. Prescott of the Thirteenth New Hampshire Volunteers remembered being "massed in the darkness of the woods awaiting the order to cross." Secrecy and silence were carefully observed. "The men were allowed to converse only in low tones, and the exhibition of any light, however small, was strictly forbidden. Meanwhile the pioneers were busy covering the bridge thickly with earth, that the measured tread of the troops in crossing might not be heard by the enemy."[62]

By 3:00 a.m., Ord's men began to cross. George Stannard's division led the way, with Hiram Burnham's brigade in front. Two of Burnham's regiments, the 10th New Hampshire under Colonel M.T. Donohoe and the 118th New York under Lieutenant Colonel George F. Nichols, exchanged their muskets for Spencer repeating rifles as their officers quickly trained them in "the mechanism of the guns as they hurried swiftly on." They were the first over the bridge, acting as skirmishers.[63] Whether owing to the security precautions or the fog hanging over the river, they initially encountered no resistance.[64] A few moments after daylight, they were one mile inland and made contact with the Confederate pickets and drove them "on the run," while suffering few casualties. The Federals continued on, and "after pushing them back on their reserves, we continued to drive them at a brisk trot through the dense woods for a distance of two or three miles with few casualties on our side."[65]

Lieutenant Prescott wrote, "The first faint flushes of dawn were just appearing in the eastern skies when the entire force found itself safely transferred to the north bank of the river, and without delay was immediately ordered forward." As they advanced up the Varina Road, they helped themselves to the breakfasts left behind by the retreating defenders, eating them as they marched on.[66] After pushing the Confederate defenders up the Varina Road for several miles, Donohoe's men reached a clearing. In the distance across an open field, they could see the daunting ramparts of Fort Harrison.

The Confederates had initially been unaware of Ord's movements.[67] Taylor remembered pickets, who had been stationed about a mile closer to the crossing, "hurried before daybreak to the Bluff and reported the enemy were crossing the river."[68] A message was quickly sent to General Ewell, who telegraphed Braxton Bragg and General Lee that the pickets had been driven in. Lee responded quickly, and by 6:30 a.m., he had ordered three of Charles Field's brigades to come up from the Petersburg area. Unfortunately for Ewell, it would take most of the day for them to arrive. An hour later, Lee called out the Richmond local defense troops and sent a message to Ewell to "encourage the men to fight boldly."[69]

When word of the Federal advance reached the camps at Chaffin's Farm, Major Taylor jumped into action. He was soon "surprised to see that the woods about a half a mile from us across a level field were filled with Yankee soldiers deploying into line preparatory to starting a charge on Fort Harrison." With little time to spare, he "shouted to the men to put their muskets against the trees" and load the guns as quickly as possible. Taylor said there were two eight-inch Columbiads and four thirty-two-pounders.[70]

While the split Confederate high command of Gregg and Ewell had guessed incorrectly about possible Federal objectives by assigning most of their troops to either end of the line, Taylor was in the middle, facing the real threat with few resources. He called to the troops that were nearby. Lieutenant John Guerrant's thirty-five-man Goochland Artillery unit was ordered to man the heavy guns. Others manned the works on either side of the fort. Regiments of Benning's Brigade headed to Fort Harrison at the double-quick.

As Taylor prepared to defend the fort, Gregg, on the left of the Confederate line at New Market Heights, was mired in a struggle of his own with Birney's Tenth Corps. He quickly realized how vulnerable the center of the Confederate line was and began sending men to Fort Harrison. He immediately ordered the First Virginia Reserves under Major James Strange to the area, and Strange placed his men to the left of the fort. Captain Cornelius Allen and his Lunenburg Artillery were nearby in Battery X. Still, Taylor had a total of perhaps eight hundred men in the area to face a Federal force up to ten times as large as his own. By any military reasoning, his was a desperate situation. Richmond was only eight miles to the rear, and Fort Harrison was the key to the defenses. Its loss would put the capital in the greatest peril it had yet experienced. Could reinforcements arrive in time?[71]

As the Federals approached the field between the Varina Road and Fort Harrison, they paused. General Burnham reported to Stannard that there was a strong line of works to his front with a number of heavy guns. Ord took a few moments to reconnoiter and then ordered his First Division under George Stannard to push forward across the open distance to the fort. Heckman's division was to move to Stannard's right, along the edge of the timber on the side of the Varina Road, staying under cover until he was opposite the fort and then attack it on the east front. Together Stannard and Heckman would envelop the fort. Once Harrison was taken, they could then clear the other strong work (take Fort Gilmer from the rear) that protected the approach to Richmond.[72] To prevent soldiers from stopping during the attack to fire their weapons, the Federals officers had the priming caps removed from all of the muskets, and bayonets were fixed.[73]

Stannard's Second Brigade under Hiram Burnham was to lead the assault. Prior to the war, Burnham had been a lumberman and a coroner in Maine. With the outbreak of hostilities, he helped to recruit the 6th Maine Infantry and became its lieutenant colonel. He took part in the Peninsula Campaign of 1862 and in May 1863 was wounded at Fredericksburg during the Chancellorsville Campaign. The following April, he was promoted to brigadier general of Volunteers and took part in the Battle of Cold Harbor.[74] On this day, three of his regiments were in front. The 21st Connecticut

Hiram Burnham. *LOC.*

was on the left, the 118th New York in the center and the 10th New Hampshire on the right. Colonel Michael Donohoe of the 10th led this group. Immediately to their rear was the 96th New York, followed by the 8th Connecticut.

To Burnham's left rear was Stevens's brigade, with the 13th New Hampshire, 81st New York, 98th New York and the 139th New York arrayed in column. To Burnham's rear right was Roberts's brigade, consisting of the 58th Pennsylvania, 188th Pennsylvania, 92nd New York and the remainder of the 21st Connecticut. They were formed in column,[75] in supporting distance of one another, and marched toward the fort across 1,400 yards of open killing ground, the land having been cleared of any trees in order to provide the defenders an unobstructed field of fire. Stannard's formation provided great power aimed at a compact target, ideal for the situation.

As they began to advance, "all at once the high walls of Fort Harrison came into view, occupying a very high crest of land, a strong natural position, nearly a mile distant." The large guns in the fort were joined by the fire of the Confederate gunboats in the James. The attackers knew that whatever had to be done "must be done very quickly," and yet they had to cross nearly a mile of open ground. One soldier remembered thinking, "The prospect is terrible."[76]

Confederate captain G.W. Breckenridge with the Second Battalion Virginia Reserves was moving up and recalled, "As we came in sight of Fort Harrison and filed right to reach the line of fortifications, I had to stop for a moment to gaze spellbound on the grandest spectacle I had ever imagined. The mile or more of open country in front of the fort was blue with Yankees advancing in column." He remembered the big guns of the fort "belching forth as their fires [*sic*] of shot and shell." As the Federals approached, "puffs

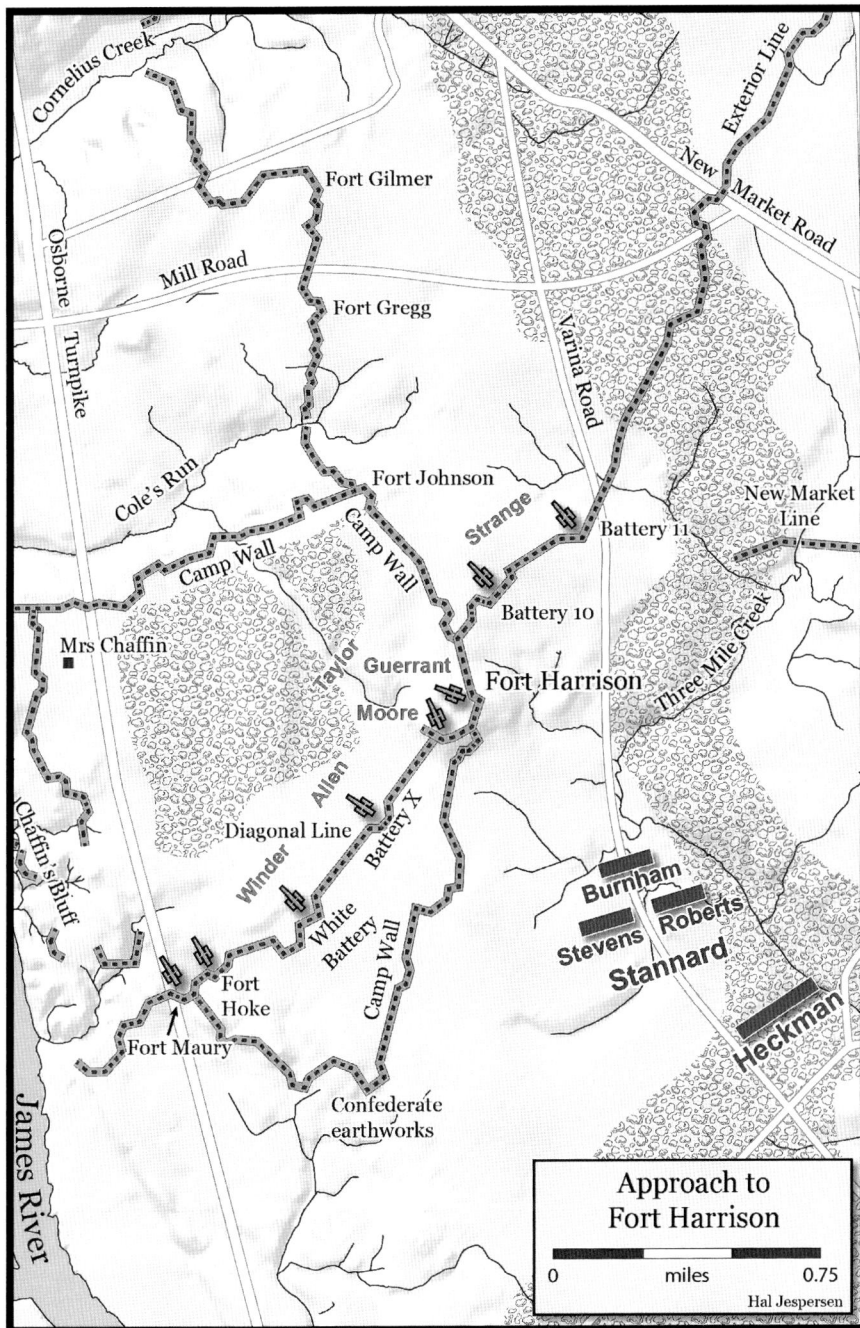

Approach to Fort Harrison. *Hal Jespersen.*

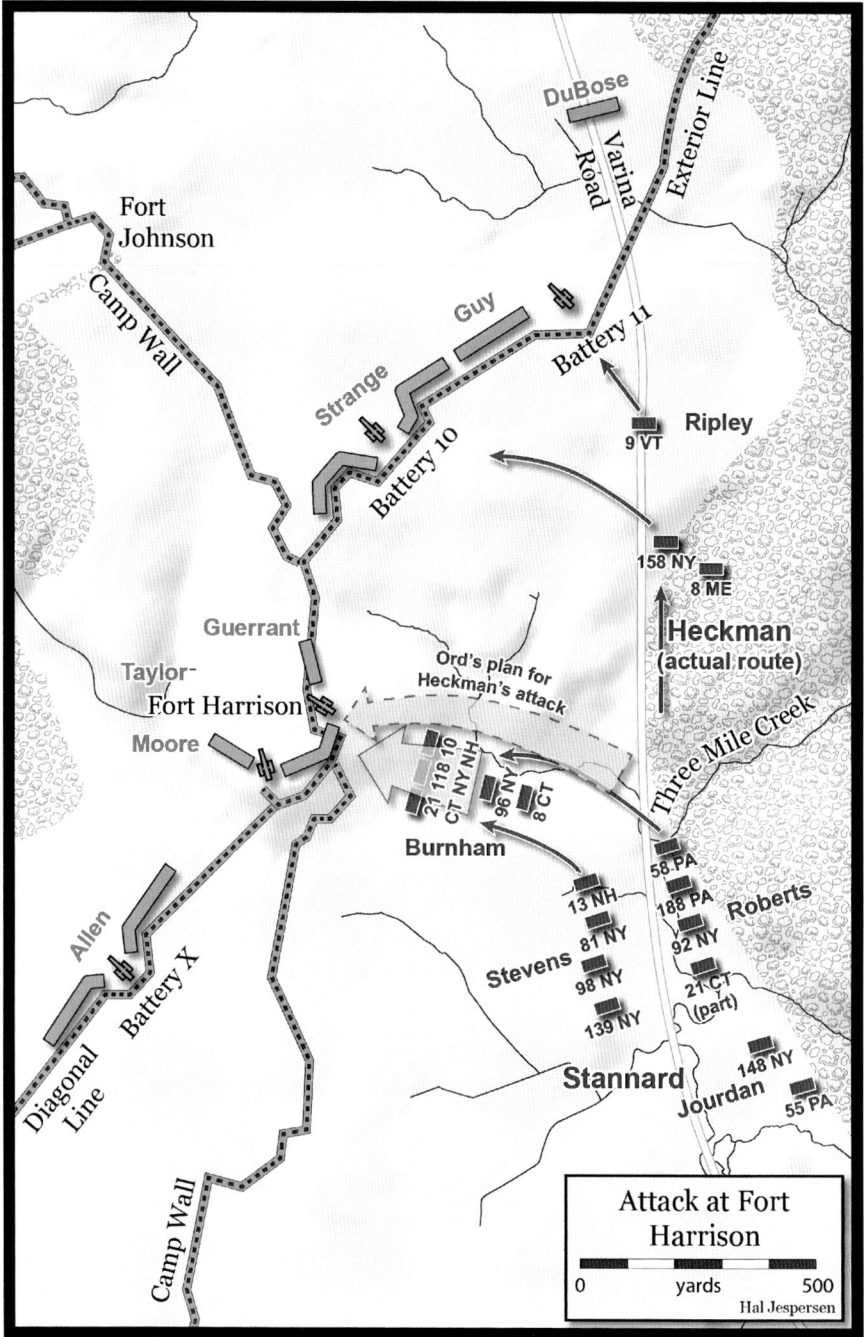

Map of the attack at Fort Harrison. *Hal Jespersen.*

Stannard's attack. *Massachusetts Commandery Military Order of the Loyal Legion and the U.S. Army Military History Institute.*

of white smoke from the muskets, the steady dress parade step of Yankees as march [*sic*] up 'e'en the cannon's mouth."[77]

The first few rounds went over the Federals' heads, but soon the Confederates had found the range and began to tear into the bluecoats' ranks. "A loud roar, a sudden burst of flame and smoke from the fort, announced that the action had begun. The first few shells screamed harmlessly overhead, only cutting off the tops of the trees and bursting behind us, but the enemy soon obtained our range and more serious results followed." An artillery wheel nearby was hit, and the shell "straightened its heavy tire and laid it flat as a ribbon along the road." Men and equipment were not the only ones to feel the weight of Confederate iron. The same shell glanced off the wheel, and then it "cut off the forelegs of a horse attached to the gun next behind, causing the poor beast to pitch suddenly forward upon its breast. Passing it, killed two more horses, and finally exploded in a group of men, killing three and wounding several others."[78]

The guns of Harrison were joined by artillery from either side of the fort, pouring a converging fire into the attackers.[79] A federal soldier saw "huge shells come tearing and screaming up from his gunboats on our left flank; the redoubts to the right and left plunge in their cross-fire; while Fort Harrison, directly in our front, plies us with shrapnel, solid shot and shell, and as we approach." As the attackers neared the fort, "rebel riflemen shower upon us their hail of lead…some of our men fall rifled with bullets; great gaps are

Stannard's attack at Fort Harrison. Wartime sketch by William Waud. *LOC.*

rent in our ranks as the shells cut their way through us, or burst in our midst; a solid shot or shell striking directly will bore straight through ten or twenty men." The terror was unforgettable: "Here area some men literally cut in two, others yonder are blown to pieces."[30]

A soldier of the Thirteenth New Hampshire Volunteers remembered the shelling by a six-inch Rodman gun:

> *As we were advancing during the assault, a shot from it had plunged into our column to my left, and I watched the Rebel gunners as they re-loaded it; saw them step back, and the puff of smoke as the lanyard was pulled. I was exactly in line, and in the centre of the flame there seemed to be a little black ball coming directly toward me. I gave a warning cry and sprang to the right—a thing that I could easily do, being then in the line of file closers—and a moment later Reuben L. Wood, a recruit in Co. G, who was directly in front of me when the gun was fired, was struck squarely in the centre of the body, the shell passing through him and flying on its way. Strange to say that the shell did not knock him over backwards, but cut a round hole in the back of his overcoat…and so true and clean was the circle cut, that apparently there was not a fragment of the cloth half an inch in length left projecting into it. He fell on his left side, terribly perforated.*[31]

Stannard's Attack at Fort Harrison, as seen from the Varina Road. A latter-day painting by Henry Clow. *County of Henrico, Virginia Historic Preservation and Museum Services.*

General Stannard recalled the defenders firing "furiously from a powerful battery situated at the crest of the hill in my front and from other guns mounted in smaller redoubts situated at various points along the line." His force was about 1,400 yards from the fort, "and while traversing this space my command, with the exception of my skirmishers, not having yet discharged a musket, was exposed to a plunging fire of artillery and musketry, galling in the extreme, and caused them to become somewhat broken." His men remained determined, and "the column, however, pushed gallantly forward until it reached the base of the hill upon which the batter was situated, when it came to a halt, from sheer exhaustion."[82]

Colonel Aaron Stevens, leading the First Brigade, was cut down by a severe hip wound that would end his army career.[83] His men continued through the killing field: "Despite the carnage in our ranks, our Division [*sic*] moves forward with wonderful steadiness, though many of our skirmishers and the assaulting column are all merged in a body together…the men need no urging, were never more ready for a fight." The enemy fire was taking its toll, as the ranks constantly "need closing and correcting in line as they are broken up by the constant falling of the killed and wounded." About one hundred yards from the fort, "the enemy's fire is so terrific that the wasted and shattered column wavers a little—the task seems impossible."[84] Another Union soldier remembered, "It looked as if we couldn't make it," but the veteran leader Hiram Burnham inspired confidence and encouraged his Second Brigade on.

Lieutenant Prescott of the Thirteenth New Hampshire remembered the advance: "Steadily, almost as if on parade, in close column by division, with arms at right shoulder, the brigades moved onward, and as the cannon shot from the fort and gunboats ploughed great gaps through their ranks, quickly closed up and pressed forward as rapidly as the nature of the ground would permit." They continued along the "mile of death." As they arrived in the shadow of the fort, they reached a point where the ground rose and the guns of the fort could not be depressed sufficiently to do further harm; "a momentary halt was made to enable the men to recover their breath."[85]

Inside the fort, Major Taylor saw that the enemy was closing in. He kept up the fire. "Our shells were mowing them down; canister and grape shot from Young's company were making lanes in them. Their officers were waving their swords and cheering them on, pointing to a valley reaching which they would be under cover from our fire. We were now double loading with grape and canister." Too soon for Taylor, the attackers reached the depression where they were safe from his large guns. "The advance of the Yankees was in a valley our of our sight I never saw the end of them."[86]

The Federals made an oblique movement slightly to the right and continued on until they reached a rise in the ground that gave them shelter. They took a moment to rest and prepare for the assault up the walls of the fort. They were safe for the moment, as the Confederate guns could not be depressed enough to hit them. It was a short, clear run to the ditch in front of the fort. As historian Richard Sommers remarked, the Confederates' "folly of failing to build a glacis during the long months of ease now became all too apparent."[87] This would have provided a sloped field of fire, allowing no zone of safety for the attacking force.

A veteran of the Thirteenth New Hampshire commented on the Federals' move to the right: "Seeing the oblique into this little ravine they evidently thought we were intending to follow the ravine and taken [sic] them by the left flank—their weak spot, and really the key to the battery, as it was open to the rear and they could have used but few of the guns against us." He noticed "a body of infantry double-quicked down to the left (our right) to head us off. But such was not our intention." He witnessed another Confederate mistake. "Their gunners must have become rattled, for just as the last man of the division reached the shelter of the ridge they fired the Rodman gun, double shotted with grape. It tore through the turf and shrieked over our heads without hitting a man." The attackers felt tremendous relief at being spared, and "a great cheer rushed up the slight rise, enheartened by seeing the Rodman gun pointing skyward at an angle of thirty degrees. The heavy and harmless charge had dismounted it."[88]

As the Union troops paused, Gregg's Confederates were hurrying on their way from New Market Heights. "Having received word that Fort Harrison was threatened; they rushed to its rescue. It had to be saved from capture or the Texans would risk being cut off from Richmond." J.B. Polley of the Texas Brigade said, "To be cut off from the Confederate Capital was to be forced to surrender or die in the last ditch."[89]

Major James Moore, in command of the Seventeenth Georgia, recalled the defenders' desperation: "Our ammunition by this time was run very low, and consequently our firing had almost ceased." The pause was deceptive, only being the "calm preceding the gathering storm about to burst upon us." The Federals rose up and began to mount the works, but Moore's men "had made every preparation to give him a warm reception, having loaded our small arms and doubles shotted with grape the 32 pounder." When the lanyard was pulled, the effect was "exceedingly destructive." A swath of destruction tore through the Federal ranks, "tearing a lane of some thirty feet or more" through the attackers.[90]

Chapter 4

Storming the Ramparts

The men of the First Division huddled under the cover of the protective ravine for a few moments and then rushed a short distance to the outer ditch of the fort, where once again they were shielded. Samuel Roberts paused to survey the scene. In the distance, he could see Gregg's Confederates quickly approaching from the east. Roberts decided that this was the moment and said, "Come boys, we must capture the fort…now get up and start!" They "almost instantaneously obeyed the command, and the column suddenly sprang forward as one man."[91] All three brigades sprung into action. Thrusting their bayonets into the walls of the fort, they clambered up, or climbed on one another's shoulders. Soon they were on top of the wall in overwhelming numbers. As they looked straight down into the "sallow, savage" faces of the enemy, hand-to-hand fighting erupted.[92]

R.B. Prescott said, "So near were they to the enemy that many were severely burned by the flame from the latter's rifles, and their faces were blackened by the unburnt powder. The fire was literally in their very faces." A Confederate gunner was preparing to fire one of the large guns into the attackers when a Union soldier yelled, "Don't fire that gun." Ignoring the warning, he reached to pull the lanyard but "fell dead, transfixed by a Union bayonet."[93] Federal troops quickly turned the gun on the retreating defenders. A veteran recalled, "The first lieutenant of the 96th N.Y. Volunteers…was going over the top of the works, but was met by a 'Reb' with his gun ready for him. The lieutenant did not have time to draw his revolver, but on the instant, he picked up a pebble from the top of the parapet, threw it at Johnnie

Storming the Ramparts, by Gilbert Gaul, used with permission of the owner. It evokes the drama of an attack on fortifications such as Fort Harrison.

and hit him squarely between the [e]yes. He instantly dropped his gun and ran." Elsewhere in the fort, "Michael Finigan, of our regiment, held a rebel colonel at point of bayonet, and ordered him to get up on top of the parapet and give three cheers for the Union."[94]

Union casualties mounted. Colonel Stevens went down, as did Lieutenant Colonel Nichols of the 118th New York. General Hiram Burnham fell mortally wounded as he led his brigade into the fort. Lieutenant Taggard of the 13th New Hampshire recalled that he was standing near Burnham when the general was hit. As the ball penetrated the general's stomach, "he placed his hands over the wound exclaiming: 'Oh! Oh! Oh!' spun around a moment, then fell."[95] The brave veteran commander died soon afterward.

When a Union soldier took a moment to look back, he would see the field behind them "covered with prostrate forms, while the groans and shrieks of agony that came to our ears were most appalling." It seemed a miracle that any of them had made it to the fort in one piece. "What with the fire from the fort and the redoubts that flanked it on the right and left, the huge shells which came screaming up from the enemy's gunboats on the river, the bullets from the enemy's riflemen posted in treetops, the roofs and chimneys of the scattered farmhouses, and from the line of rifle-pits, it is a wonder

Capture of Fort Harrison, a latter-day painting by Sidney King. General Burnham receives his mortal wound, top center. *RNBP.*

that the column was not completely annihilated." The lack of abatis was a stroke of great fortune for the Federal attackers. L.B. Prescott later stated, "Had their been an abatis in front of the fort, it is certain that it could not have been taken, and why so important a position was unprovided with this valuable protection is something I have never been able to understand."[96]

Men strove to be the first to plant their colors on the fort. The entire color guard of the Thirteenth New Hampshire was killed or wounded, "four of them with colors in their hands."[97] While many of the outnumbered and often inexperienced defenders fled, some stayed to fight. Colonel Maury rode up to the fort and was informed by Taylor of the desperate situation. Guerrant's gunners picked up rifles and pistols and fired away at the Federal horde. Major James Moore of the Seventeenth Georgia "gave the order to get out in the best manner possible and re-form at the next line of works." Still some defenders remained defiant. Moore recalled that Private A.P. McCord was "on the top of the traverse embankment firing down into the midst of the enemy, not more that fifteen feet distant." He remained in this position "until the bluecoats became as thick within the works as blackbirds upon a millet stack."[98] A Confederate officer rode out a sally port and pulled up on the bridge spanning the ditch and blazed away with his revolver.[99]

Taylor later wrote, "The Columbiad near which I was had just fired a fearful dose of missile, when some half dozen heads behind glistening gun barrels appeared on a traverse some twenty feet away, and gave us a volley, dropping several men at the guns, myself among them." As his men tried to hold on, "a number of Yankees were coming in from the rear of the fort. Two of them handed down from a pole near me our flag, and ran up the stars and stripes."[100]

Cecil Clay, captain of Company K of the Fifty-eighth Pennsylvania Infantry, remembered:

> *The first two men of the brigade who mounted the parapet were Billy Bourke, of Co. B, 58th Pa and I. We climbed up high enough to look over and see a number of men standing ready to fire, when a shot struck Billy across the forehead, he fell over against me and we both rolled back into the ditch. The blood ran into Billy's eyes so that he could not see, and I then took from him the blue state flag of the 188th Pa., which he had carried when we first climbed the parapet...I received two wounds while on the parapet, and when I jumped down on the banquette, a third. I stopped Serg't Nathaniel McKown of Co. B, 58th Pa. and asked him to cut off my gloves and sleeves and see how much damage had been done. While he was doing that I stood the flag against the parapet...I carried in the first color.*

Captain Clay's wounds proved to be so serious that his arm had to be amputated. He was later awarded the Medal of Honor.[101] As Clay grasped the Pennsylvania colors, William Graul grabbed the national flag from the hands of the dead William Sipes. He climbed the parapet and planted it.[102]

William Graul was eighteen at the time of the attack. He had enlisted as a private in Company I of the 188th Pennsylvania in 1863. Wounded at Cold Harbor, he, along with his regiment, was one of the first to reach the works at Fort Harrison. Graul was to live and have five children, with his son Randolph inheriting the Medal of Honor he won this day. Captain Theodore Blakely, a three-year veteran with a wife and three children, was thirty-three years old when his men charged the fort. He was "struck in the side by a ball and fell; but quietly rising to his feet he, sword in hand, urged forward the men to the charge, when a ball passed through his head, causing immediate death."[103] Such acts of individual heroism were common that day, but sadly most have passed long forgotten into history.

Colonel Maury was soon captured by the enemy, as was Taylor, who was severely wounded as his men were overwhelmed.[104] Some of the defenders took shelter in the barracks at the back of the fort. Here the Thirteenth New Hampshire used their rifles "for the first time." In the close hand-to-hand fighting, "the bayonet has won this battle." Their enemy had not had time to eat their breakfast, so the Federals "heated, hungry, begrimed with powder

Theodore Blakely. Used with permission of the owner.

smoke and dirty…enjoyed their enemy's breakfasts in their stead and arose feeling obliged to them for it."[105]

Hopelessly outnumbered, and with Federals coming in all around them, the defenders retreated to nearby entrenchments, hoping to stem the Union tide. The Second Georgia took up position at Fort Johnson, about a half mile from Harrison. With fewer than one hundred men, and running short in ammunition, word was sent that they needed ammunition or they would be forced to withdraw. A.P. McCord and John Lindsey volunteered to go back to the cabins that had been abandoned to the enemy and attempt to retrieve whatever they could carry. Each succeeded in getting a box of cartridges and returned, "under a heavy fire some half mile to Col. Shepherd's men." Major James Moore went to the aid of Shepherd and, finding that he had been wounded, took command.[106] Could they and other Confederate defenders hold the line until enough help arrived?

Stannard's First Division had taken control of the fort, but at a heavy cost. All of the division's brigade commanders, and some of their replacements, were out of action. Many other field officers were lost, as were staff members. In addition to the loss of brigade commanders Stevens and Burnham, Colonel Roberts, already ill, succumbed to his sickness and had to relinquish his command. Stannard reported that 8 officers were killed and 36 were wounded, with 550 enlisted men being killed or wounded.[107] The chaos of the attack, combined with the loss of leaders, led to confusion inside the fort, and it would take some time to sort things out and continue the assault. It was still early in the morning, and the door to Richmond was ajar. The Union had never been presented with this great an opportunity to take the Confederate capital, but the opportunity, however great, was fleeting. Lee would not likely ignore this threat to his capital for long. Time was of the essence. Ord looked to his Second Division, under Charles Heckman, to continue the assault from the right. Confederates still manned many of the smaller fortifications and earthworks, and the imposing Fort Gilmer remained in the hands of the Southerners. Where were Heckman and his division?

According to Ord, Heckman had been directed to stay to the right of Stannard's division, skirting the Varina Road and staying under cover. Once he came upon Fort Harrison, Heckman was to attack it from the eastern side, enveloping the work. He then "would have been available to have attacked the only other work which intervened between us and Richmond in the rear."[108] This would have been Fort Gilmer, which, like Fort Harrison, was open in back. As Ord did not issue written orders before the attack, it is uncertain that Heckman was clear on this plan,[109] but Colonel E.H. Ripley, commanding Heckman's Second Brigade, confirmed that Heckman's division was to sweep to the right of Stannard, break through the Confederate lines and sweep toward Fort Gilmer and the other batteries and "take them in reverse."[110] Perhaps Heckman had failed to reconnoiter before his attack, and his men became bogged down in the brambles on the side of the Varina Road.[111] In any case, Heckman made a number of serious tactical errors that day. Failing to attack as planned and then take advantage of the open rear of the enemy forts was one of his most costly.

Could Fort Johnson's guns, about a half mile distant, have stopped Heckman if he had followed the plan? This seems unlikely, as Fort Johnson was not heavily defended, with the Powhatan Artillery arriving there only after Harrison had fallen. Even if Johnson were adequately manned, it's doubtful that the defenders of that fort could see Harrison, owing to a curtain of trees.[112]

Heckman did not wheel toward Fort Harrison, but instead his Second Division continued up the Varina Road,[113] heading for Confederate Battery 11. It soon found the woods very difficult terrain to maneuver in, filled with typical Virginia undergrowth of vines and brambles, almost "impenetrable slashing." Along with Ripley's Second Brigade, Colonel James Jourdan's First Brigade moved northward. Most of Jourdan's troops became entangled in the undergrowth along the road, and Fairchild's Third Brigade likely also became entwined. Heckman's force had thus bogged down, with only two of his seven regiments emerging to assault the enemy. One of the Second Brigade's regiments, the Ninth Vermont, managed to work its way through and went on, with little support. The regiment was made up of a number of green recruits, many who had only received their rifles within the past twenty-four hours. In the 800-man regiment, 225 men were new recruits who had joined the unit since the first of September.[111]

As they advanced, the men of the Ninth came in sight of a Confederate thirty-two-pound gun that had already caused some damage, killing a number of horses. Ripley, leading Heckman's drive up the Varina Road, was trying to bring up some of his own guns in order to support the charge he was preparing. The road was narrow, and the troops rolled the dead horses into the ditches, in an attempt to clear a passage.

I had forced my way through between the guns and was trying with him to get guns, caissons and horses doubled up enough to give my brigade a passage, when another shell from the thirty-two pound gun exploded with great havoc among the horses and men. I instantly felt the whole right side of my head tear away as I was knocked off my horse, stunned. Captain Sam Kelly, of Company B. sprang to me and sat me up when I came to my senses. I asked him, "How bad is it, Sam?" "Where are you hit?" he asked. "Is not my head gone?" "No," he replied, "it seems all right." Then slowly and timidly I put my hand up to what felt to be an awful cavity where my ear had been, and could hardly believe my senses that it felt all right to my hand. The piece of shell had clipped my hair and cap button and the windage has seemed as harsh and cruel as iron.[115]

In an effort to avoid the almost impenetrable undergrowth, Companies B and K crowded down the roadway "directly in the very mouths of the guns." With the earthworks a half mile in the distance, they began to race to the fort, with the regiment's color sergeant, Felix Quinn, leading the way. The battery had abatis in front that had to be cleared, and Private Henry French, an eighteen-year-old farmer, was accidentally pushed into one. The tree limb stabbed

Edward H. Ripley. *Massachusetts Commandery Military Order of the Loyal Legion and the U.S. Army Military History Institute.*

him, taking him out of the action, but he was able to return to his unit several months later. The bluecoats expected a blast of grape or canister at any moment, but strangely, they heard none. On the Confederate side, the men of the James City Artillery had found that the ammunition was low.[116]

As the Ninth Vermont rushed for the works, the defenders abandoned them, but not before turning to fire one last rifle volley. The Ninth took Battery 11, forcing the James City Artillery and the Twentieth Georgia to retire to the intermediate defenses.[117] Ripley turned the guns on the defenders. Quickly wounded were Sergeant Burlingame of Company K and Lieutenant Dodge of Company B. Sergeant Major Belden "had a ball enter his wrist and come out above the elbow, but with his sound arm he seized the trail of a gun" and said to Ripley, "Go on colonel, we wounded men will work these guns." John Riley, of Company B, was killed. John L. Newton was hit in his right thigh and died of complications on October 27.[118] Although he had taken the Confederate position, Heckman's effort was misguided and costly. Had he stayed to Stannard's right and then attacked Fort Gilmer, these minor works would likely have fallen without a fight.

The 8th Maine became bogged down in the dense underbrush, so the 9th had attacked alone. Soon the 158th New York of Jourdan's Brigade broke through and struck to the left of the 9th Vermont. They assaulted Battery 10, overrunning the two guns, and sought to turn them on the defenders.[119] The situation for the Confederates was perilous. The exterior line had been pierced; Fort Harrison and Batteries 10 and 11 had fallen. Fort Johnson and Fort Gilmer remained the last hope of slamming the door on the Federal offensive. If they fell, Richmond would be open to assault by Ord's Corps, with little to defend it.

As soon as General Ewell learned of the Union attack, he notified his superiors and headed out to rally the defenders. Meanwhile, Lee had to wonder if this was another of Grant's two-pronged attacks. Was one of the assaults a feint? Was Grant's real move south of Petersburg, or was it at Chaffin's Farm? Could they both be the real thing? Where would Lee's limited troops do the most good? He could not afford to be wrong. If he sent his troops across the James, Meade might cut the railroad to Petersburg and Lee's supplies from the south. If he went after Meade, Grant might overwhelm his force north of the river and go into Richmond. He had to be sure.

Once convinced that the Chaffin's Farm attack was not a feint, he responded to Ewell's warning by ordering troops from Bermuda Hundred and Petersburg to head for the north side.[120] He wrote to Braxton Bragg in Richmond and said, "Genl Ewell reports the enemy have possession of Fort Harrison. Order out the locals and all the other troops to his assistance." To Ewell, he responded with an order to retake Fort Harrison. He followed this up with another note: "Can you not draw some troops from your left to retake Fort Harrison? It will take time for troops from here to reach north side. Don't wait for them, endeavor to retake the salient at once. Pickett has been ordered to send a brigade to the north side."[121] The local defense forces, of varying quality and limited experience, were rushed out to join the line. General Field, with three brigades, was on the way from the south side of the river.[122] Lee would arrive in the afternoon to take personal command.[123]

In Richmond, the local defense forces had been called up. Men left their jobs and headed to the front. In his diary, John B. Jones recalled, "Information came that the enemy had captured Fort Harrison (Signal Hill), near Chaffin's Bluff, and were advancing toward the city. From that moment such excitement sprung up (the greatest I have ever known here), and all the local organizations were immediately ordered out." The Confederates were desperate for manpower, and "squads of guards were sent into the streets everywhere with orders to arrest every able-bodied man they met, regardless of papers; and this produced a consternation among the civilians." With men being taken away and an emergency on hand, "offices and government shops were closed, and the tocsin [alarm bells] sounded for hours, by order of the Governor, frightening some of the women."[124]

When Ewell arrived in the vicinity of the fort, he found the Federals, with an overwhelming force, in control of the works. He quickly realized that if Ord pushed ahead, he could outflank the Confederate forts on either side. Returning to his old form of his days with Jackson, Ewell established a thin line at the edge of the woods, gathering anyone he could find, including teamsters, prisoners and some available troops to display a show of force.

Richard S. Ewell. *LOC.*

Although heavily outnumbered, Ewell had the benefit of the woods behind him, so the Federals could not be sure of his numbers. Instead of attacking straight ahead, the bluecoats provided Ewell with the gift of time and turned to the south.[125] The extremely thin defenses on either side of Fort Johnson to the north had been spared for the moment. Private Charles Johnson remembered "very distinctly how he [Ewell] looked on an old gray horse, as mad as he could be, shouting to the men and seeming everywhere at once." Johnson added, "By his cool courage and presence wherever the fight was hottest, [he] contributed as much to the victory gained as any man could have done."[126] This was perhaps the greatest of all of Ewell's contributions to the Confederacy.[127]

Chapter 5

Opportunities Lost

Meanwhile, Ord had been trying to organize the units inside Fort Harrison and continue down the line of enemy earthworks with the goal of capturing or destroying the Confederate pontoon bridges,[128] thereby severing the most direct link between Ewell's forces and his main army. Ord wanted to prevent the arrival of Confederate reinforcements. His task was difficult, as Union troops were mixed and scattered, and several key leaders were down, including all brigade commanders. In following Butler's orders of September 28, Ord intended to destroy the pontoon bridge just above Chaffin's Bluff.[129]

Sorting out the confusion and organizing an attack was costing the Federals precious time, and the Confederates were making the most of it. They were pulling local units together, while Lee was busy moving reinforcements from across the James River and Gregg continued to send men from the New Market Heights area.[130] In the heat of the moment, having lost his brigade commanders and perhaps not experienced enough to overcome that challenge, Ord decided to personally lead a force and attack the line of Confederate works leading to the river, including Battery X, White Battery, Fort Hoke and Fort Maury.[131] While he headed toward the river, he was not taking advantage of the opportunity right in front of him—Fort Johnson. Should that fall, he could take Fort Gilmer from its unprotected rear and blow a major hole in the Confederate line. Heckman's Division could be the spearhead. Instead, Ord decided to concentrate his efforts on Forts Hoke and Maury. With his superiority in numbers, it is likely that he could have done both, but with the disorganized state of his corps and the loss of the First Division's brigade commanders, it was not to be. The fleeting moment of incredible opportunity was beginning to pass by the Federal attackers.

Pulling available First Divison troops together, Ord, with Colonel Michael Donohoe of the Tenth New Hampshire (now leading the Second Brigade), and Colonel Edgar Cullen of the Ninety-sixth New York (heading up the Third Brigade), drove the Confederates from Battery X and White Battery and pushed them back to their final works on that end of the line, Forts Hoke and Maury. With their backs to the wall, Captain Cornelius Allen's Lunenburg Artillery moved into the forts and helped the defenders hold, joined by men of various other detachments. Lieutenant John Winder's men braved Federal fire to pull two small six-pound howitzers out of White Battery. In addition to the guns brought by Winder, Captain Allen stated that he had "rallied seventy-five to one hundred men and held the fort." Allen also had a twenty-four-pounder and another brass howitzer. They manned the few pieces of artillery, while the remainder of the men grabbed muskets and lined the walls. He recalled, "There were no troops between us and the doomed city." They would have to desperately hold on until reinforcements arrived.[132]

To help, General Lee had ordered the gunboats of the James River Squadron to "cooperate with the army in preventing further advance toward the bluff,"[133] and the guns of the *Nansemond* and *Drewry* began firing, though without much effect. Soon the *Richmond* and the *Fredericksburg* joined in. *Nansemond* suffered from poor shells of poor quality and limited range and was sent upriver, but it was soon replaced by *Roanoke*, and together the ships fired hundreds of shells at the advancing Federals.[134]

As Ord led the attack, his men were driving the enemy when he was suddenly wounded in the thigh.[135] Despite the injury, Ord improvised a tourniquet and continued in command until a surgeon finally sent him to the rear for attention. As commendable as his personal bravery was on this day, the mounting loss of experienced leadership was beginning to weigh on the Union advance. Had they attacked with the organized strength of Stannard's assault on Fort Harrison, the defenders probably could not have held out. With Ord down and the attackers not properly organized, Confederate resistance stiffened and, combined with solid works and fire from the navy, brought the Federal attack to a halt.[136] Two more Federal officers went down: Colonel Donohoe of the 10th New Hampshire and Lieutenant Colonel Nichols of the 118th New York were both severely wounded.[137]

Before being taken away, Ord turned command of his corps over to the ranking subordinate, General Heckman, who had limited combat

Charles A. Heckman. *Massachusetts Commandery Military Order of the Loyal Legion and the U.S. Army Military History Institute.*

experience, the most significant of which came the previous spring. Personally brave, he was not gifted tactically. He had been captured at Drewry's Bluff and exchanged during the past month, then he chanced into a division command with the Eighteenth Corps. Now he fell into an even greater assignment, one for which he was ill prepared. Ord ordered him to gather the available forces near Fort Harrison and attack the works toward Richmond in succession. Ord was deeply concerned that the First Division had exhausted its ammunition and that Confederates could be expected to be coming from across the river at any time.[138]

Upon being given command of the corps, Heckman approached Colonel Ripley, and the latter said he "seemed to have become crazed" and ordered Ripley to advance from Battery 11 and attack Fort Gilmer. Rather than go around behind the fort, as he had understood the original plan, Ripley was to attack it directly. To the colonel, "this was madness." The Tenth Corps, which could offer support by attacking Fort Gilmer from the east, had not arrived. The brigades of Jourdan and Fairchild, "which were needed for supports, were entangled in the swamps some distance back." With his small force, he was to attack a fort "as strong as Fort Harrison or stronger, and fully manned."[139]

Ripley took the available troops, the Ninth Vermont and portions of the Eighth Maine, and began to advance, but they were met with fire from both Forts Gregg and Gilmer. "Shells from the forts cut swaths through the regiment." A shell fragment hit Private Daniel Dwyer, taking off most of his right hand and tearing into his thigh. Private James Lunge was hit in his cartridge box, tearing away flesh from his abdomen and hip. Both men survived. Private George W. Patrick was not so fortunate. A shell fragment killed him, leaving a wife and four children without support, other than a very small government pension. Private Freeman Baker was struck and "blown to atoms" by a shell from Fort Gilmer. Convinced that the attack was a "wicked waste of life," Ripley ordered his men to fall back. "For several hours they lay…with white hot pieces of iron flying around or overhead. Most closed their eyes and tried to imagine themselves somewhere else or cried or prayed to God to be spared."[110]

While they were enduring the enemy shelling, Ripley was looking though his field glasses, analyzing the situation, when a private from a Massachusetts battery would jump up after each explosion. Ripley told the man to stay down three or four times. As a shell exploded nearby, the man jumped once again, and Ripley was hit with a disgusting mass. Another soldier cleaned Ripley's face, and they looked to see the headless form of the jumping man, whose brains had been splashed on Ripley.[111]

As he moved past a spot where another shell had exploded, Ripley saw a pitiful sight. He looked down to see the dreadfully wounded William Moranville of Company E. The twenty-year-old corporal was lying on his side. The young man's body was mangled; his buttocks down to his thigh were "carried away showing a raw mass of torn flesh with the crushed bones protruding." Still conscious, Moranville weakly requested water. Ripley gave the corporal some from his canteen, but Moranville showed more anxiety toward his colonel's safety than his own injured condition. He implored Ripley to seek shelter and not concern his welfare. The colonel departed but first promised to send a stretcher. When he located one, he ordered it sent back to the desperately wounded man, but the Confederate fire made that nearly impossible. "Captain Kelley, of Company B, with volunteers, tried several times to reach Corporal Moranville and the other wounded, but did not succeed until night, only to find him dead."[112]

The Confederates, too, displayed great heroism. Badly outnumbered everywhere, they had fought all through the morning, giving ground, but thus far the Federals had failed to break through their lines and advance on Richmond. They raced from position to position, always staying one step ahead of the attackers. At Fort Hoke, Captain Cornelius Allen led the defense. He was wounded in his right hand and left arm, and then a bullet ricocheted and struck him in the chest. As he was carried away, he ordered Lieutenant Jugurtha Laffoon to "hold his guns to the last minute and the last man."[113]

After the Federals had taken Fort Harrison and its adjacent batteries on the outer line, some of the Confederate defenders rushed to Fort Johnson. It was the key work between the forts on the river and Fort Gilmer and would need to be taken to allow an attack on Fort Gilmer's rear. Confederate colonel Dudley DuBose realized the importance of holding this position, and the two hundred men he had were veterans. If it were lost, the entire line

Fort Johnson. Notice the depth of the ditch (see the man standing at the rear of the picture) to prevent Federals from digging a mine. Also notice the row of abatis to the right. *RNBP.*

could be compromised. Captain Willis Dance and the Powhatan Artillery set up quickly and began firing, joined by DuBose's Georgia troops. Fortunately for the Southerners, Heckman did not carefully plan this important attack, and as a result, it was very poorly coordinated, with amazingly few troops getting into the action.

Those brave souls who did attack were faced with dismal prospects. They had to advance across an open field, subject to the defenders' fire all the way. Near the fort, a line of abatis stood. The Confederates had also laid out a series of land mines (actually artillery shells adapted to explode when something pressed down on them). If the attackers somehow survived and got past these obstructions, they faced an extremely deep ditch, dug low to prevent the tunneling of a Federal mine, like the one attempted the past July at the "Crater" in Petersburg. On the other side of the ditch were very high ramparts. A frontal assault on a position like this was ill advised; a weak attack against it was suicidal.

The remainder of Jourdan's Brigade finally arrived on the scene and was now available, but it was used ineffectively and was not supported by other available units. Once again, rather than maneuver and attack a weaker part of the defensive line and get in the rear of Fort Johnson, Heckman decided to attack a position head-on. Again he failed to take advantage of his overwhelming numbers and attacked with small units rather than massing his troops.[114] He was giving the defenders, brave as they were, every advantage they could hope for. Colonel Harrison Fairchild led the Second Pennsylvania Heavy Artillery, followed by the Eighty-ninth New York, and they began their three-quarter-mile approach to the attack. They advanced under a shower of bullets and shells. "A shell struck the ranks of my company, killing Joseph Spence and wounding 12 men," wrote John Alexander of the Second Pennsylvania. "One comrade had to have the mainspring of a gun cut out of his breast where it imbedded itself." Alexander saw Allen Egglestin of West Pittston, Pennsylvania, lose his hand. As he was placed on a stretcher, Egglestin said, "Boys, tell my mother I died in front of the rebels." The soldier was "not yet sixteen years old."[115]

Major James L. Anderson led his battalion within one hundred yards of the works until he was decapitated. One of the Confederate guns was silenced, but three more continued firing away at the approaching blue line. Members of the Second Pennsylvania's First Battalion finally reached the moat and became trapped, and the Second Battalion fired in support, but the Eighty-ninth New York retired before it could provide support. Another Pennsylvania unit, the Third Battalion, was too far to the north and was halted by the guns firing from Fort Gregg. Some of the trapped men of the First tried to storm the ramparts but were too few in number, and most were either shot or taken prisoner. Georgian defenders counterattacked the left flank of the Second Battalion, driving it away and isolating the remaining survivors of the First. Fort Johnson remained in Confederate hands and was to become a key to the new defensive line. The repulse of this assault, like the ones at Forts Maury and Hoke, bought the Confederates more desperately needed time.[116]

Around eight-thirty that morning, General Grant heard the news that New Market Heights had fallen to Birney's troops, and he left his headquarters at City Point to visit the front and see things for himself. Satisfied that the Tenth Corps had things well in hand, he headed for the left wing to see the results of Ord's attack. He barely missed Ord, who, although wounded, had left the area searching for Grant or Butler so he could plead for reinforcements, artillery and a new commander for his corps. To Grant, the appearances at Chaffin's Farm were very impressive. Imposing Fort Harrison had fallen, as had several of its associated works. Union troops seemed to be on the move against the Confederate lines. He probably did not see that the Federal attack was not properly organized and had lost its momentum. Ord was wounded and was away searching for Grant, so the latter likely did not clearly understand the situation. Heckman apparently did not provide information on the state of affairs.[117]

About 10:00 a.m., General Grant arrived at Fort Harrison. He looked about, then "sat down on the step of a small traverse…the nearest small traverse to the south side of the great traverse." Grant reached in his pocket and pulled out paper and a pencil "and commenced writing a dispatch on his knee." As he was writing, "a large shell—the kind the soldiers call a 'three-gallon demijohn'—came up from a Confederate gunboat on the James, passed with a howl very near over Gen. Grant's head, and with a loud thud struck on the side of the great traverse." It was in the direction that Grant was facing, and "directly in front of where he was sitting, rolled down into the open space towards him, and stopped within a few feet of him, the fuse still burning and threatening an instant explosion." The other soldiers lunged for cover "in various parts of the works, and a number instantly laid flat upon the ground," but General Grant did not appear fazed. He "sat perfectly still, merely looked at the shell a moment, and then resumed his writing, all as unconcernedly as if nothing unusual had occurred. The shell, however, did not explode, though there was every reason for expecting that it would do so at any moment."[118]

During the morning, Grant received a dispatch from Lincoln. The president was concerned that Lee would send reinforcements to Early and was reminding his army commander of that. The Union commander sought to ease Lincoln's mind by stating that he had taken "steps to prevent Lee sending re-enforcements to Early by attacking him here." Some strong works had been taken as well as several hundred prisoners.[119] Grant also wrote to Major General Halleck in Washington, informing him of the victory at Fort Harrison: "General Ord's corps advanced this morning and carried the very strong fortifications and a long line of intrenchments [sic] below Chaffin's Farm…General Ord was wounded on the leg, though not dangerously." He also remarked that things also looked positive in the Tenth Corps' sector, where "General Birney advanced at the same time from Deep Bottom, and carried the New Market Road and intrenchments [sic] and scattered the enemy in every direction…he is now pushing on toward Richmond."[150]

Being unclear of the true status of the Eighteenth Corps, Grant optimistically wrote to General Birney, telling him that Ord's force was ready to advance "in conjunction with you," and to "push forward on the road I left you on" (the New Market Road).[151] It is unknown if he provided any instructions to Heckman, but unfortunately for the Federals, it appears that he did not. As Grant set off for Deep Bottom, so did the last chance that day for a strong, concerted attack against the weak Confederate center.[152] Before leaving, Grant complimented Stannard on the performance of his division but was impatient as to the whereabouts of the commander of the Army of the James, General Butler, who had overall responsibility for the day's offensive. Ripley commented, "General Grant rode away with an expression of great annoyance and contempt." Later, Butler finally appeared:

> *We saw a large cavalcade come dashing along the Varina road, up which we had come in the morning. This was about 4 P.M. It was easily recognized as Major General Butler, the commander of the Army of the James, which had been fighting since daylight and had just ventured up to see what was going on. He came dashing toward us. No large shells had fallen since he had passed out into the opening of the woods. The boys began to laugh and to prepare to see him turn tail as soon as the gunboats opened again, and they prayed devoutly for them to do so quickly. At last the dull angry roar rolled up again from under the bluffs of the James. Butler pulled up from his gallop to a trot. Another roar, and from his trot to a walk, and other and his walk to a halt. For a moment he sat, with his arms akimbo on his hips, taking in the scene with a melodramatic air and turning tail he walked a little, trotted a little and then broke into a gallop…glittering staff and dashing escort all plunged out of sight from whence they came and we saw them no more.*[153]

Heckman repeatedly squandered his units in piecemeal attacks rather than massing troops for one strong push. He attacked Batteries 10 and 11, as well as Fort Johnson, head-on, when he could have forced them to be abandoned by strong, concerted attacks. He had not taken advantage of the fact that the Confederate forts were not enclosed; they had no protection to the rear. Grant had failed to understand the true situation, and Butler was absent. Either could have exerted influence on events. The cost to the Federals was high. Out of the roughly 8,000 men Ord brought across the river, 1,273 were killed, wounded or captured during the campaign, with most of those losses occurring in the attacks of that day.[154] Of critical importance was the high cost in leadership, from the corps commander down to the lower field leaders. It was a high butcher's bill, and it could have been worth the terrible cost, but as it was, it was only half a victory.

While Ord's Divisions under Stannard and Heckman were heavily occupied at Chaffin's Farm, his other division, under Charles Paine, had been loaned to the Tenth Corps for this campaign and was involved in the assault on New Market Heights. In that sector, a few miles east down New Market Road, Paine's USCTs were not only involved, but they were also spearheading the assault. These troops demonstrated extraordinary courage. They were attacking fortified Confederate lines with abatis placed in front of the defensive works, with spaces in them prearranged so attacking troops would naturally gravitate toward them and attempt to funnel through. When they did, they would be greeted by pre-sighted defensive fire, which could lead to appalling losses. If that were not enough, they were black soldiers. Other USCTs had been captured in an action at Fort Pillow (on the Mississippi), and those who surrendered were reported to have been massacred. The real possibility existed that if they were captured they could meet the same fate, or they could be forced into slavery. For them, the risks were particularly grave.

The USCTs attacked with courage. Many were heroic. Several grabbed flags that had fallen and tried to rally their comrades. Holding the flag was critical, for in an age with no battlefield telecommunications and a field dominated by black powder smoke, it was difficult for units to maintain their cohesion. Flags were the visible rallying point for each unit. Of course, they were the obvious target for the defenders and were among the first to be targeted. Other USCTs rallied their men and led the charge after the white officers had fallen (USCT units did not have black officers). For their bravery, the USCTs at New Market Heights were awarded fourteen Medals of Honor.

The USCTs prevailed and took the heights. An argument can be made that Confederate general Gregg, who commanded the defenses in the sector, was pulling his men away in order to hurry to the defense of Fort Harrison just as the final Union attack at New Market Heights was made. This is certainly plausible, but it does not diminish the incredible bravery displayed by the USCTs. If people of the North questioned their ability to fight, the answer was given at New Market Heights and would be reinforced later that day at Fort Gilmer.

Chapter 6

Assault on Fort Gilmer

S trategically, Grant's original plan to launch assaults on both ends of the line to threaten Lee and to prevent him from sending reinforcements to Early had not only worked, but it had also seemingly achieved a breakthrough that was exceeding his expectations. On Grant's left, Meade was poised to attack the next morning. On the right, Butler's offensive had driven the Confederates from New Market Heights and had taken their strong position at Fort Harrison, and they seemed poised to capitalize on these and break through to Richmond. It appeared to Grant that Ord's force would soon be able to link up with David Birney's, and consequently Grant had ordered Birney to push on down the New Market Road toward the Confederate capital. At 12:50 p.m., Butler wrote to Grant that they were going to try to take the remaining enemy works, and "if they are carried it is the last obstacle." The latter responded by saying, "You will see that all must be done to-day [*sic*] that can be done toward Richmond."[155] Unfortunately for the Federals, things are not always as they seem.

Veteran Confederate forces were beginning to appear. Gregg's men continued to arrive from the New Market Heights area. During the morning, Union signal officers had been writing to Butler, advising him that wagon trains and troops in railroad cars were heading for Richmond. Following Lee's instructions, Pickett had sent a brigade across the river, but instead of sending one entire brigade, he had taken one regiment (the Twenty-fourth, Thirty-second, Fifty-third and Fifty-sixth) from four Virginia brigades and placed them under the command of Colonel Edgar Montague. The colonel reported to Ewell at 1:00 p.m. Upon command from Lee, Field had set off immediately with Law's Alabama brigade, taking time only to grab ammunition, a canteen and a few biscuits.[156] Also, senior leadership was arriving; Major General Richard Anderson finally appeared and met with Ewell around 11:00 a.m.[157] Lee himself was on his way.

The Federal Eighteenth Corps was spent. Heckman was now leading the corps, and he had squandered the morning's promise with his ineffectual, piecemeal, head-on attacks. Nearly half of Butler's assault force was now basically taking on a defensive role. David Birney's Tenth Corps, accompanied by Paine's Division of the Eighteenth Corps, was still advancing down New Market Road, heading for the intersection with the Varina Road, where it expected to meet Ord. However, the men of the Tenth Corps had already had an exhausting day. Following a long march the previous afternoon and evening to reach the bridge to Deep Bottom, they crossed the river before dawn, then marched and attacked New Market Heights.[158] After taking the Heights, they then marched approximately three and a half miles toward the intersection with the Varina Road. These were hardly fresh troops, ready to attack. Regardless, if there was to be a Union breakthrough to Richmond, it would have to be accomplished by Birney's men.[159]

Birney's troops passed the junction of the Varina and New Market Roads. Approximately a quarter mile past that intersection, the Confederates had placed a battery of twelve-pound Napoleons at Laurel Hill Church. To drive off these guns, Union troops attacked the Laurel Hill position but soon began receiving fire from the two large guns positioned at Fort Gilmer, about one mile to the south. That fort had a ten-foot moat with two lines of abatis on its northern side. It also held two large sixty-four-pound guns.[160] Like Fort Harrison, it was vulnerable to the rear. Gilmer was the largest

David B. Birney. *Massachusetts Commandery Military Order of the Loyal Legion and the U.S. Army Military History Institute.*

Confederate bastion remaining, and it was second in importance only to Fort Harrison. It became readily apparent that Fort Gilmer must be reduced if the Federals were to continue past Laurel Hill and into Richmond. The closest troops Birney had available were those of Foster's Second Division, and they were selected to make the assault. Foster's Division had been seriously weakened that morning and contained only about 1,400 troops out of an original 3,600.[161] Nonetheless, Foster received his orders at 1:25 p.m. and was informed that William Birney's brigade was to advance on his left, with support from Paine's Division of the Eighteenth Corps.[162]

The Confederates reacted quickly to the threat posed as Foster's men took the works at Laurel Hill. General Gregg moved the Texas Brigade just to the west of Fort Gilmer. One of his veterans remembered, "I venture to say that we made that half mile in about as short a time as men ever passed over the same distance. Panting for breath, we took position in the intrenchments [sic] to the left of the fort…we were just in time."[163] DuBose moved to the right with the Twentieth Georgia, and Captain Madison Marcus had an assortment of some two hundred troops inside the fort.[164] In addition to its two heavy guns, Gilmer had a few pieces of field artillery available. The Confederates also had guns from the Louisiana Guard Artillery that were stationed on the Intermediate Line that could enfilade any Federal movement toward Fort Gilmer from the Laurel Hill area. Additionally, there were several others in nearby Fort Gregg.[165] The troops and guns were few, but with a moat and abatis, an attack on the fort could be a very costly venture.

Foster, who had been told that he would receive support on his left from Birney, was to advance within ten minutes of receiving the order. With little time to prepare, he formed his line, with Colonel Galusha Pennypacker's brigade on the right. Colonel Rufus Daggett's brigade was in the center, and Colonel Louis Bell's was on the left. Foster had limited experience as a division commander and formed his men as a line, rather than massing them as Stannard had done when he attacked Fort Harrison,[166] reducing the effectiveness of their attack. His men moved out at 1:35 p.m. They had to cover a distance of between three-quarters and one mile, over ground that contained several ravines, as well as underbrush that had been slashed and laid out as obstructions.

There was a cornfield between the final ravine and the fort, with an open field of fire for the defenders. They came under fire from Fort Gilmer, as well as from the Confederate artillery manning the intermediate line, to Foster's right.[167] These would hit Foster during the entire movement, and resistance would only get stronger as his command approached the fort. If supporting

Robert S. Foster. *Massachusetts Commandery Military Order of the Loyal Legion and the U.S. Army Military History Institute.*

fire did not come from another direction, all of the defenders' available fire would be directed at them.

Foster's men went through the first ravine, but the undergrowth and slashing, combined with the Confederate artillery fire, was causing casualties, and the attack was losing order. Daggett's Brigade was hit as soon as it emerged from the woods, and things quickly got worse. "As the lines went forward, the severity of the fire increased…shells were made to explode just above and in advance of the first line, while grape and canister were used with frightful effect. Soon a withering musketry was superadded."[168] They continued on, enduring intense fire, with men falling all around. The artillery was taking a horrific toll, with the bodies of some men completely severed in two. "A piece of shell struck the musket of a soldier of the 117th New York with such force as to double it and drive it through his body." Another soldier was cut in two. They continued on.[169]

Foster ordered a halt to re-form in the second ravine. They then advanced to the third ravine and "after reforming the last time, the line moved forward to the assault and advanced rapidly under a heavy fire." Added to the infantry fire was that of the artillery. The attackers faced the "fire of grape and canister from Fort Gilmer, and shell and case from the two forts to the right," and they fell back. Grape and canister were basically containers packed with large iron balls that were released and scattered as soon as a cannon was fired, much like a huge shotgun. Facing it was every soldier's worst nightmare. Shell and case were projectiles that exploded in the air, raining down pieces of the iron shell, and case shot contained a load of small iron balls. They tore flesh apart; the men were butchered. Despite the carnage, Foster's men re-formed and attacked again, only to be repulsed once more. More defenders joined the fray. Foster remembered, "As my line

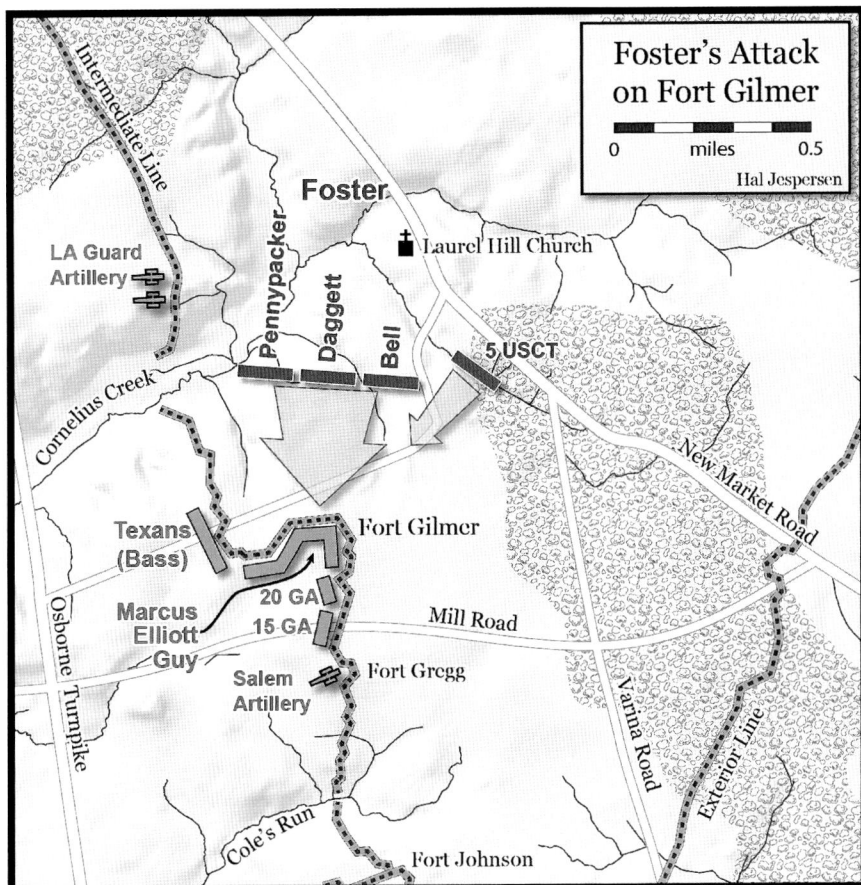

Foster's Attack on Fort Gilmer. The Fifth USCTs were not in the first attempt. *Hal Jespersen.*

advanced to the assault a body of troops of the enemy, apparently 500 or 600, moved from the fort on the right, and reached Fort Gilmer in season to assist the garrison in our repulse."[170]

Lieutenant Colonel Albert M. Barney later recalled the attack, saying, "The brigade moved on the works across a ravine thickly covered with slashed timber." This created some confusion, but they continued on. "The progress of the brigade was not interrupted by the fire of the enemy until it reached a second ravine, in advance of the first about 350 yards." A battery on the right soon opened on them, with effect. As they rose out of the second ravine, they were hit with musketry, "which continued growing more severe as we advanced toward a third ravine." They went down into the ravine and

Bell's troops prepare to attack Fort Gilmer, with the Fifth USCTs coming up to support. William Birney's USCTs can be seen waiting on the left. Latter-day painting by Henry Clow. *County of Henrico, Virginia Historic Preservation and Museum Services.*

were afforded some protection, but that was fleeting: "On rising the hill, over the third ravine, the column was opened on by a galling fire of grape and musketry from the left, that swept down the men by dozens, under which the line advanced some fifty yards." They continued their attempt: "Some of the men got to within twenty-five yards of the abatis, but they were unable to stand the fire." The officers tried to hold the men steady, but "the line fell back in some confusion as far as the church, where it was reformed."[171]

On the Federal left, Louis Bell's men had also met stiff resistance. One of Bell's veterans looked at the ravines to be crossed, the downed trees, the abatis, the fort's moat and high walls and said, "What was our astonishment and terror when we received orders that we would charge those forts…it looked like suicide to attempt it." Regardless of their concerns, attempt it they did. Bell's five regiments formed and then advanced toward the fort, instantly shelled with "great violence." They began to run, "tearing

Attack at Fort Gilmer. Daggett's men (left) and Pennypacker's (right) are coming out of the third ravine to attack. Latter-day painting by Henry Clow. *County of Henrico, Virginia Historic Preservation and Museum Services.*

through the underbrush and fallen trees, shot and shell screeching around our heads." When they crossed the third ravine, they faced the flat, open ground between them and the fort, and the Confederate fire grew stronger. Try as they might, they could not advance through the fire. Sixty men in one of Bell's regiments, the 115th New York, began the assault. Five men were killed, and twenty-four were wounded, with four missing. Over half of the unit became casualties.[172]

Numbers don't tell the whole story. Each man advancing toward the fort experienced his own personal hell. As he rose out of the second ravine, Captain William McKittrick of the 115th New York, who had fought as a teenager in the Mexican War, was hit by a shell and killed. Lewis Bertrand, a thirty-four-year-old private who had just returned to the unit after being wounded in the head at Cold Harbor, was shot through the head and died. Charles Spiegel ran to Bertrand's aid and was hit in the chest. He managed to crawl to the to the safety of a tree stump and survived but never returned to the 115th. Sergeant Charles Fellows carried the regiment's flag into the battle and was hit in the leg by a bullet. Captured soon thereafter, Fellows had his leg amputated by a Confederate surgeon. Freed by his captors, Fellows never recovered and died on November 11.[173]

From the Confederate side, A.C. Jones saw the imposing Federal force: "There must have been a full brigade, probably fifteen hundred or two thousand men. In two lines they came, sweeping down upon us." The defenders tried to make every shot count, before the attackers could reach them. "Those Arkansas men did good shooting you may well believe, and with every shot there went up a Confederate yell to emphasize their aim." The Federals, rising from the last ravine, felt the sting of their fire. "No doubt those Yankees thought as they came down the slope that they were facing thousands instead of about one hundred Arkansas ragamuffins. Our fire was deadly, and many of them fell; but on they came." The attackers kept coming, but the defenders held their ground. "At about twenty-five paces I emptied a navy revolver from my left hand, my right arm being disabled by a wound. At about ten paces one of their color bearers went down, and then the line broke and dissolved." The Confederate fire had the desired effect: "For a while the field seemed full of bluecoats running for life, followed by the parting shots and exultant shouts of our men."[174]

As their casualties mounted, the Federals tried to care for their wounded. A Union veteran remembered: "The wounded were taken to a dwelling about half a mile to the rear, which with the yard and outbuildings was used as a hospital. Soon every foot of available space about the premises was occupied. Men were borne in with every conceivable form of wound. A number were wounded in two or more places."[175]

Foster rallied his men and, joined by the Fifth USCTs, they advanced. Lieutenant Grabill of the Fifth remembered, "It was a mad enterprise, but it was ordered." They advanced "through a front and cross fire of artillery, through two ravines and slashing of brush and trees." They continued on "through the brigade of white troops which had been badly repulsed, and even went beyond the point they had reached." Increasingly, a sense of the "utter hopelessness of succeeding pervaded the mind of everyone." Soon the attack broke, and "companies one by one" rose, "as if collecting themselves," and they walked "deliberately from the field." Another lieutenant saw a "sergeant who had received three wounds crying because the battalion would go no farther."[176]

Foster's command lost 35 killed, 309 wounded and 119 missing in their attempt to take the fort, but to no avail.[177] The Confederates stood defiant.

Although once again greatly outnumbered by their attackers, they held their position, and their efforts had bought time for reinforcements to make it up from Petersburg. General Charles Field's men began to arrive, led by the Alabama brigade of Evander Law. They had been shipped by train to Drewry's Bluff and then had double-quicked the five miles to Fort Gilmer, taking only short breaks to walk and catch their breath. As fiercely as the Confederates had fought, they were fortunate indeed that once again a Federal commander had not attacked with more of the troops at his disposal. William Birney's assault that was supposed to support Foster's had not yet begun. It is unclear why David Birney did not coordinate the attacks of Foster and William Birney. His orders to Foster indicated that Birney's attack was to be simultaneous with his own, but he soon received instructions to start within ten minutes of receiving the order.[178] This hardly left the time needed for coordination. It is also possible that he was feeling pressure from Butler, who had set up his headquarters on New Market Road, just east of the exterior line. At 12:50 p.m., Butler wrote to Grant and said that Birney was "at this moment making his attack."[179] Whatever the reason, Birney's order left little time for coordination and had the effect of dooming all of the attacks to failure. Once again, the defenders could focus all of their wrath on an attack coming from a single direction.

The Federals' effort was not yet done. Although Foster's men had been repulsed before they reached Fort Gilmer, the Union troops were going to make another effort to storm the works. On the eastern side of the fort, David Birney's brother was crossing the Varina Road and preparing to attack. William Birney had a total of five regiments but left two of them out of the fight. The Forty-fifth U.S. Colored Troops had only recently arrived, so Birney did not allow them to join the assault. The Twenty-ninth Connecticut was also a USCT unit, and Birney held it in reserve. The attack would be made by the Seventh, Eighth and Ninth USCTs. Birney's lack of brigade-level experience was quickly evidenced, as instead of massing his three regiments for attack, he sent them forward in piecemeal fashion one regiment at a time, often further diluted by attacking several battalions at a time.[180]

William Birney first hurled Captain Edward Babcock's Ninth USCTs against the southern end of the fort. Babcock described the action in his report: "The regiment moved by your orders into the woods on the left, thence across a small road (understood to be the Mill road) and formed in a shallow ravine to charge a redoubt of the enemy's, distant about 1,500 yards." Captain D.G. Risley led four of the companies (C, G, K and E) forward as skirmishers, while the remainder advanced in line of battle. They began the charge as soon as they reached the crest of the ravine and were "immediately subjected to a very severe artillery fire, enfilading the line on both flanks. After advancing about half way to the point of attack, finding the distance unexpectedly great, the men exhausted, and the line somewhat

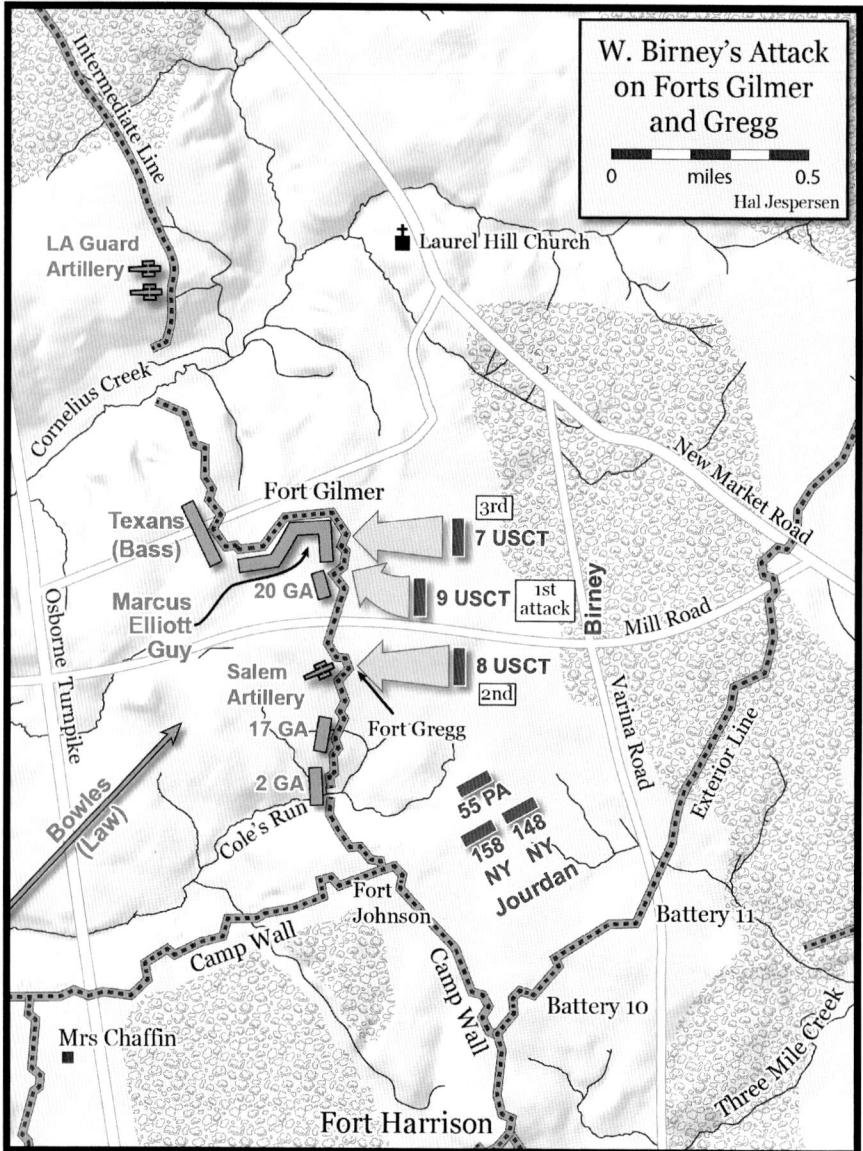

Map of Birney's attack on Fort Gilmer. This attack was supposed to be launched in conjunction with that of Foster. *Hal Jespersen.*

shaken, I ordered the regiment to halt, lie down, and reform." Babcock returned for additional instructions and was ordered "to attack the fort which enfiladed us to the right. This however, was already attempted by Capt. H.S. Thompson, commanding in my absence, who felt compelled to return the regiment under grape and canister poured into it from this work."[181]

Birney next decided to send the Eighth USCTs against Fort Gregg, a short distance to the south of Gilmer. Major George Wagner had eight companies but only about 250 men to launch the attack. They were fired on by the remaining big gun at Fort Gilmer, the Salem Artillery's four twelve-pound Napoleons at Fort Gregg and a three-inch rifled cannon from Fort Johnson. DuBose's Georgia Brigade added its small-arms fire. Wagner's men bogged down, and he was soon convinced that to continue would be "to have them slaughtered and still make no impression on the enemy's position." He reported this to his commander and said that he would continue if so ordered. William Birney responded by telling him to hold the line where he was, and the attack of the Eighth USCTs ground to a halt.[182]

The piecemeal attack was continued by sending in the men of the Seventh USCTs under the command of Colonel James Shaw. The advance of the Eighth had been stopped, and its men had retreated as the Seventh emerged from the woods, just to the right of where the Ninth had attacked. Shaw received orders from William Birney "to form in 'right into line' on the right of the road and in a direction oblique to it, a slight descent in the ground partially covering the line, then to charge and take an earth-work some three-quarters of a mile in our front." Before forming his line, Shaw received another message, which in his mind seemed to countermand the previous one. "I was directed to send out four companies as skirmishers for the same purpose. Companies C, D, G and K were designated for this purpose, Capt. Julius A. Weiss, the senior captain, in command."[183]

The verbal orders Colonel Shaw received were not clear to him, and he apparently interpreted them as meaning that he was only to attack with four companies. He questioned the orders and received a reply from Birney's adjutant, Captain Marcellus Bailey: "Well, now the general directs you to send four companies, deployed as skirmishers, to take the work." Shaw obeyed the orders as he understood them and sent forward four of his companies, leaving his remaining companies in the rear.[184] Following the battle, Bailey wrote to Shaw, stating, "The brigadier-general commanding has no recollection of having countermanded the first order mentioned by you. The only subsequent order from him was given to you by Captain Bailey, his assistant adjutant-general." He went on to say that he had created a memorandum of the order: "The general commanding directs you to advance with your whole force and attack the work in your front, which is firing. You will throw forward four companies of your command as skirmishers."[185]

The truth surrounding the orders to Shaw will probably never be known. What is important, and instructional, is how important clear orders are and how, in the confusion of battle, a misunderstanding can lead to tragic results. Could Shaw have taken the works with his entire regiment? That is difficult to say, but it does not appear likely. In any case, the USCTS, whom many had thought would not make good soldiers, proved at Fort Gilmer, as they had earlier that day at New Market Heights, that they could indeed fight. In David Birney's several disjointed attacks on the fort, they made it the farthest but paid a heavy price for their courage.

Captain Julius Weiss led the 9 officers and 189 men of the Seventh USCTs into the cornfield, and they were soon met with a devastating volley of grape, canister and rifle fire. The attackers did not stop to return the volley but instead double-quicked and raced toward the fort. No abatis blocked their way as they ran toward the fort's moat,[186] so the way was clear, but the defensive barrage was devastating. A Confederate officer described the scene, stating that the way they "fell before it was very gratifying to the people on our side of the works."[187] A soldier, Jess Lott, remembered, "While we were fighting we would run to different angles in the fort and take aim, rise up, and fire at the same time."[188]

The men of the Seventh advanced until they reached the deep moat of the fort, and in an effort to scale the walls, "many of them got upon the shoulders of others and attempted to crawl into the fort, but our boys were standing with loaded guns and when one put his head above the ground he lost that head and went back to the ground dead." Captain Weiss recalled that as they attempted to scale the walls, muzzles of the enemy guns were "almost touching the storming party," and the defenders received them "with a crushing fire, sending many into the ditch below, shot through the brain or breast."[189]

One of the USCTs took refuge behind a tree stump and fired an occasional shot. Seeing this, Confederate "Captain Griffin ordered that the stump be given a solid shot. Just as Charlie Jones had placed the shot in the muzzle of the gun, and stepped back, the negro [sic] fired from his stump and the bullet passed directly through Charlie Jones' chest, and he expired in a few minutes." The cannoneers continued with grim determination. "The friction primer having been inserted, and I, holding the lanyard, was ordered

Ditch at Fort Gilmer where the Seventh USCTs attacked and were trapped. *RNBP.*

by the gunner to fire. The gunner's aim was so accurate that the stump was torn in pieces and the negro killed and left lying there."[190]

A leader of the attack, Sergeant Green, "was killed behind the cord wood." Another, who was called Corporal Dick, "did not have a hair on his head; it was so slick it reminded me of a Virginia onion." The corporal "was one of those who got upon the shoulders of another negro [*sic*] and made an effort to come over into the Fort; he was shot between the eyes and fell back into the ditch to sleep." In an early version of hand grenades, "our boys took shells and set them up on the breastworks" after putting a very short fuse in them and "lit them off with a match and rolled them off into the ditch among the negroes. They would explode about the time they struck the bottom of the ditch and you can judge the result that followed their explosion." This soon caused the remaining attackers to surrender. "Many lying on the ground were unhurt, and seeing our men approaching, made a dash to escape; but of the many who attempted it we saw only two or three succeed. There was a well about forty feet deep just in front of Fort Gilmer and our boys removed the curb, filled the well with dead negroes, putting Corporal Dick at the bottom."[191]

An observer recalled looking down into the ditch: "They are shot in the head, the heart, and wherever it is fatal to be struck. All staring upwards— some with sullen faces, others with a surprised look upon them; some with their hands clutched, but most with arms and legs extended, as if in peaceful repose." An artilleryman nearby said, "That fellow you see lying just there was bending over one of them [the lighted shells] to pick it up and throw it back at us when it exploded and blew the top of his head off."[192]

Bravery knew no color or uniform. "A white officer of one of the negro regiments was mortally wounded and begged piteously for water. Captain (John H.) Martin heard the cry and went beyond the line to a well, which was exposed to the fire of the enemy and got water for the wounded Federal officer. The Yankees opened a severe fire upon him, but he persisted until he had drawn the water and fulfilled the scriptural injunction 'give thine enemy drink.'"[193]

Only one of Weiss's men returned to the Union lines uninjured, and forty-seven were later rescued from the cornfield. Weiss's battalion was essentially wiped out.[194] Of those captured, many were met with hatred by the Southern defenders. Jess Lott stated, "It was the only time during the war that I felt like shooting prisoners." One was claimed as a slave, some were executed on the spot. Hearing of this, General Ewell ordered that this must stop and that the captured soldiers should be treated as prisoners of war. They had proven their courage and that they could fight as good as any soldiers.[195] Instead, they were "consigned to the slow death of prison, where two-thirds of the survivors eventually perished."[196]

Birney's disjointed attacks failed to dislodge the defenders, and the cost was fearful. Of his brigade, 430 men were killed, wounded or taken prisoner. Of these, 235 were from the Seventh USCTs. Their commander, Colonel Shaw, remarked, "We lost the four companies almost entire [*sic*]."[197]

As the fighting at Gilmer ebbed, General Heckman ordered James Jourdan to attack Fort Gregg. This isolated attack was typical of his efforts throughout the day. Richard Sommers aptly noted the "tragic consistency" of Heckman's leadership, describing him as "the officer who could not co-ordinate his first attack with Stannard's, who could not co-ordinate his own brigades with each other, and who could not co-ordinate the elements of the corps that had passed under his command."[198] Heckman once again failed to coordinate, this time with the attacks on Fort Gilmer; consequently Confederate fire from Forts Gregg, Gilmer and Johnson could be concentrated on Jourdan's troops. The men of the 148th and 158th New York flanked the 55th Pennsylvania as it spearheaded the attack, but as Heckman remembered, "Almost the instant I made the attack the firing on the part of the Tenth Corps ceased, and the firing of these three forts was at once centered on my brigade in addition to a heavy infantry fire on our left flank, compelling our force to retire. I am now holding the old position waiting further orders."[199]

With the repulse of this attack, large-scale fighting in the Fort Harrison area quieted down for the evening, but to the south, at Fort Hoke, things heated up again. The Confederates who had defended the fort earlier had turned it over to less experienced troops. Stannard had been ordered to attempt to get close enough to the pontoon bridge to destroy it with artillery.[200] Edgar Cullen's brigade charged the fort, and the poorly trained defenders abandoned the works. The Union victory would prove to be short-lived. Fort Maury still remained in the way of any advance toward the James River bridges, plus there was the matter of the Confederate gunboats in the James, a short distance away. Stannard began to pull his men back to the defensive line that was being built. They attempted to spike or carry away the captured guns, but before they could finish, the Confederates, led by Edgar B. Montague, struck the fort and recovered the works. The Southerners then re-took Battery X. Montague then began to head for Fort Harrison. Stannard's Division, with Napoleons from Battery H of the Third New York Light Artillery, blocked their way with shell and canister. Montague could go no farther. Any additional fighting would have to wait for the morrow.[201]

At 3:50 p.m., Grant had written to Butler that it might be advisable to hold the ground for the night and "feel out to the right in the morning."[202] Butler responded at 9:10 p.m., stating that he was holding the works taken during the day but asked if General Meade was going to attack below Petersburg. If not, he requested that Grant send him another corps, as he feared that Lee would send troops across the James and threaten his rear.[203] The night would prove to be an uneasy one. To protect their gains against a Confederate attack, Union engineers General John G. Barnard and Lieutenant Colonel Cyrus B. Comstock began laying out a line from Cox's Ferry on the river to Fort Harrison and then to New Market and Darbytown Roads.

After nightfall, the men of Heckman's Division moved to the left of Fort Harrison. Soldiers of Ripley's Ninth Vermont took part in building a new defensive line. The troops were worn out by loss of sleep, and after marching and fighting all day, they were ready to drop at any minute. "The instant we halted, the men dropped in their tracks as though shot. In a few moments along would come the order 'side step to the right and close a gap with such Brigade' [sic]. We would kick, prick and pound the almost insensible men up, and side-step, halt and drop." Rest was not to be had, as "then would come another order from the other direction, 'side step to the left' or 'march forward' or 'backward' until at last we got the engineers satisfied and thought we were going to sleep." Their work was still not finished. Instead of being able to stop and rest, "shovels and pickaxes were passed along, and

View of Fort Beauregard (in the distance) from Fort Burnham (Harrison). *LOC.*

we dug like beavers all night, until by morning for two miles or more we presented to the enemy a fairly strong breastwork with five redoubts in it manned by light batteries."[204]

Whatever the awareness or competence of his superiors, George Stannard was a good enough soldier to know that he would have to strengthen his defenses and that the Confederates might well try to take back their works. After sunset, Stannard sent out a large picket line, consisting of about half of his remaining troops, while the remainder labored to enclose the rear face of Fort Harrison.

Ready to drop from exhaustion, Stannard's men knew what was at stake and continued to work, throwing up a breastwork using any materials they could find and trying to close the open back of the fort until they were temporarily relieved. Around 9:00 p.m., Heckman ordered him out of the fort, and Stannard lined up his troops just outside the left wall of the fort, extending toward the river with his left end turned back, or "refused," in order to repel any Confederate counterattack. One of the desperately tired soldiers wrote, "At nightfall, worn out with loss of sleep, hard marching and excitement, the men longed and looked for rest, but instead were taken down to the south slope of Fort Harrison and in the darkness and rain which began to pour, weary hours were spent in trying to get alignment for a new line of works."[205]

Bomb-proof in Fort Burnham (Harrison). *LOC.*

"A strong rifle-pit, with log traverses, had been thrown up on the left and along the center." Timber, logs, barrels, boxes and bales of hay were used to strengthen the defenses, but unfortunately "the right had no such protection." They worked with bayonets, sticks and even coffee cups.[206] At eight o'clock on Friday morning, Stannard's men returned to the fort. "A rifle-pit had been dug two-thirds of the way across the rear, which had now become the front."[207] The defenses thrown up to the rear of Fort Harrison would prove to be invaluable the next day, but they were not complete. There was still an open space to the right. The men continued to work, and the "gap was somewhat lessened, and the breastworks straightened, during the forenoon, in spite of an incessant fire of shells which was maintained from the guns in the enemy's second line of works, and of 'pots and kettles' from his gunboats in the river, while his sharpshooters picked off all who exposed themselves outside the trenches."[208]

Over the long night, the Federal forces prepared for the counterattack they expected the next morning. Stannard was limited mostly to infantry, as the heavy guns had been removed from the fort and shipped across the bridge at Aiken's Landing. He did have Michael Donohoe's 10th New Hampshire and the 118th New York and their Spencer breechloading rifles, which could put out a lot of firepower.[209] H.E. Baker of the 118th New York perhaps put it best when he said, "We expected them on the morrow, for they were very angry on bidding us good-night."[210] When Stannard and his troops were ordered back into the fort, he placed his men carefully, with the breechloaders in "double lines behind the low curtain, while the artillery was arranged as well as the difficult nature of the ground would admit."[211] Things would remain quiet until midday, with the exception of the nine-inch shells lobbed over from the Confederate James River Squadron, which fortunately did little damage.[212]

The surgeons were busy as well. Dr. Erastus P. Fairman, sent to Fort Harrison immediately after its capture, was the first surgeon to arrive, and he set up a small hospital in the grass in a hollow near the fort. He and other surgeons performed amputations "until it became too dark to operate,"[213] all the while with "shot and shell from rebel gunboats flying over our heads."[214] The Confederate defenders also had a difficult night, not only preparing defenses and readying for the next day's action, but also stealing moments to grieve over their fallen brethren. "As night spread its mantle over the bloody scene, and brought quiet to the contending forces, the men of the Jeff Davis Artillery had time to give attention to their fallen comrade, Charlie Jones. A grave was dug in the rear of, and near a redoubt, beside the Mill road, and his body laid to rest, with a prayer by one of his comrades, B.F. Ellis."[215] This was a scene repeated over and over in the Chaffin Farm area on the night of September 29.

Chapter 7

Lee Strikes Back

O nce Lee decided that he could not ignore Butler, he moved swiftly. General Pickett was ordered to send a brigade across the river. Charles Field sent the brigades of Bratton, Anderson and Law north by rail to a pontoon bridge, where they disembarked and marched across the river and then up to the front. General Hoke sent his brigades: Johnson Hagood's South Carolinians, Colquitt's Georgia Brigade, Clingman's (under Hector McKethan) and Kirkland's North Carolinians, plus Scales' Brigade from Wilcox's Division. Porter Alexander brought artillery, and by the morning of the thirtieth, he had thirty-seven guns in the vicinity.[216] Lee came over himself to take command of the action.

Lee wanted to attack immediately on the twenty-ninth and drive the Federal forces back from Fort Harrison, but this was not practical. When Ewell was asked to attack, he wisely waited; he didn't yet have the strength he would need to launch an assault with any hope of success. It would take time for reinforcements to arrive, and time was precious. Logistics was a major problem. There was only one railroad to carry troops from the Petersburg front to the Richmond area, and it had very limited capacity. Lee had ordered the construction of an additional pontoon bridge, which was completed in time for Hoke's men to cross. No matter how badly Lee wanted to attack on the twenty-ninth, he had to wait as the reinforcements competed for their turn on the train. Even with the railroad, there was additional marching to be done in order to get to Chaffin's. The units Ewell did have on hand were of mixed quality. Some were hard-fought veterans; others were city

Charles W. Field. *Massachusetts Commandery Military Order of the Loyal Legion and the U.S. Army Military History Institute.*

clerks who had never fired a shot in anger. Most were exhausted from the action of the day. An attack on the twenty-ninth would not be wise. While some of the troops from south of the river made it over during the afternoon, many did not arrive until during the night or the next morning. Lee and Ewell would have to wait.[217]

About 11,700 Confederates had crossed the river by the morning of the thirtieth, and they joined with the 4,100 already in the Chaffin's Farm area and another 4,600 around Richmond. Butler had lost some 3,000 men during the fighting on Thursday and had roughly 21,000 effectives remaining.[218] Seven of Lee's brigades were fresh, while Butler's men were exhausted from marching on the twenty-eighth, fighting on the twenty-ninth and digging most of the night. Lee also had a first-rate commander for the artillery in Porter Alexander. As he planned the attack, Lee made provisions to safeguard his right flank toward the river. Bass, DuBose, Scruggs and Elliott were sent to man the intermediate line in that direction. Gunboats on the James would provide further protection.

On the thirtieth, Lee had about one-quarter of his entire army north of the river, preparing to attack, but this was not the same army that had driven McClellan from the gates of Richmond, crushed John Pope at Second Manassas and won at Fredericksburg and Chancellorsville. It was not even the same army that had fought Grant so stubbornly all during the past summer. Tied down in the fortifications around Petersburg and short on manpower, supplies and experienced field commanders, Lee had not had many opportunities for the offensive thrusts that had been so effective in turning back previous Union armies. Opportunities to strike were now very rare. Lee felt that he had to take advantage of this chance to attack and drive the enemy away. He arrived at Chaffin's on the afternoon of the twenty-ninth to personally see that it would be done.[219] In Richmond, the editor of the *Whig* wrote on the morning of the thirtieth, "The sentiment among the officers at the front is one of confidence of the ability of our troops not only to maintain their present lines, but to reoccupy those held by them on Wednesday last."[220] Confidence aside, what would happen that day? Would the bluecoats continue their drive into the city, or would General Lee be able to throw them back?

On the evening of the twenty-ninth, Butler, fearful that the Confederates would attack him near the river and get into his rear lines, asked Grant to send him another corps. While he did not obtain the requested reinforcements, the troops of the Eighteenth Corps did receive one large break. Charles Heckman had been totally ineffective on the twenty-ninth. Realizing this, Butler acted swiftly and placed Brevet Major General Godfrey Weitzel in command of the corps.[221] Grant temporarily ordered Butler's troops to remain where they were for the present but to be ready to move if an opportunity presented itself. He still hoped his strategy would work: "It seems to me the enemy must be weak enough at one or the other place to let us in."[222] For his part, Butler was convinced that the Confederates had sent out all of their available manpower, including clerks and policemen. "We have got now before us everything there is. A few more men and we can push through."[223] For the moment, Grant was not convinced.

After dark on the twenty-ninth, General Gregg told Charles Field that Lee "wished to take Fort Harrison that night," but Field's men were worn out from the day's exertions. Nevertheless, an attack that night would reduce the time the enemy had to build their defenses. Field took the brigades of Bratton, "Tige" Anderson and Law and started out toward the fort. At 1:00 a.m., Field reported to his superior, Lieutenant General Richard Anderson, who told him he was mistaken and was not to attack that night. His troops fell back and "went to sleep on our arms. All night long we could distinctly hear the enemy in Fort Harrison hard at work strengthening it, and by the next day it had become a most formidable place." Years later, Field would consider "it a great misfortune that it was not attacked that night. I believe my division could have retaken it then."[224]

By 9:00 a.m. on the thirtieth, the Union defenses were set. Stannard was in the center, holding Fort Harrison with brigades now commanded by Moffit, Cullen and Raulston. Heckman was to his left, toward the river, with Jourdan, Ripley and Fairchild, in that order. To their left was Pennypacker, and then there was a long, thinly defended stretch to Strong's force at the river. To Stannard's right was the Tenth Corps, with the commands of Paine, William

John Gregg. *Massachusetts Commandery Military Order of the Loyal Legion and the U.S. Army Military History Institute.*

Birney, Foster and Terry extending to the north. On the army's far right, stretching to Darbytown Road, was the cavalry under Kautz. Butler realized the danger to his left flank, in Pennypacker's sector, and attempted to move troops to protect it, but it was too late as his orders were stalled in the chain of command.[225]

Lee needed to decide where to attack. Historian Richard Sommers, in his study of the battle, clearly analyzed the options open to the Confederates. Lee noticed the weakness of the Federal left flank and the opportunity that existed to turn that flank and drive them from their source of supply. The possibility existed to cut them off and destroy them, but the risks were great. Should Grant respond and send forces across the river, Butler could counterattack. Lee could be pushed to the river and could risk the destruction of a large part of his army. As daring as he was, he could no longer afford such a gamble. Striking the Federal northern flank offered some promise, but it could expose the Confederate center to renewed attacks. Lee decided to strike at the Union center—Fort Harrison.[226]

Hoke and Field's divisions would make up two assaulting columns. Hoke would come from the west, and there was a ravine that would offer protection as he assembled his troops in preparation for the attack. Field formed to the left of Hoke, with some distance between them, in the vicinity of Fort Johnson. There was to be "severe artillery fire of twenty or thirty minutes' duration," after which they were to "rush upon the work simultaneously." Field did not have the benefit of the ravine that shielded Hoke and consequently could not align his troops too close to the target.[227] When his men attacked, they would have to cover nearly one half mile, out in the open, fired on in the front by the defenders at Fort Harrison and on the flank by Paine's men. It would take nerves of steel to cross that ground.

Although they were separated and at different distances from the target, Hoke and Field were to launch attacks so they would arrive in front of the

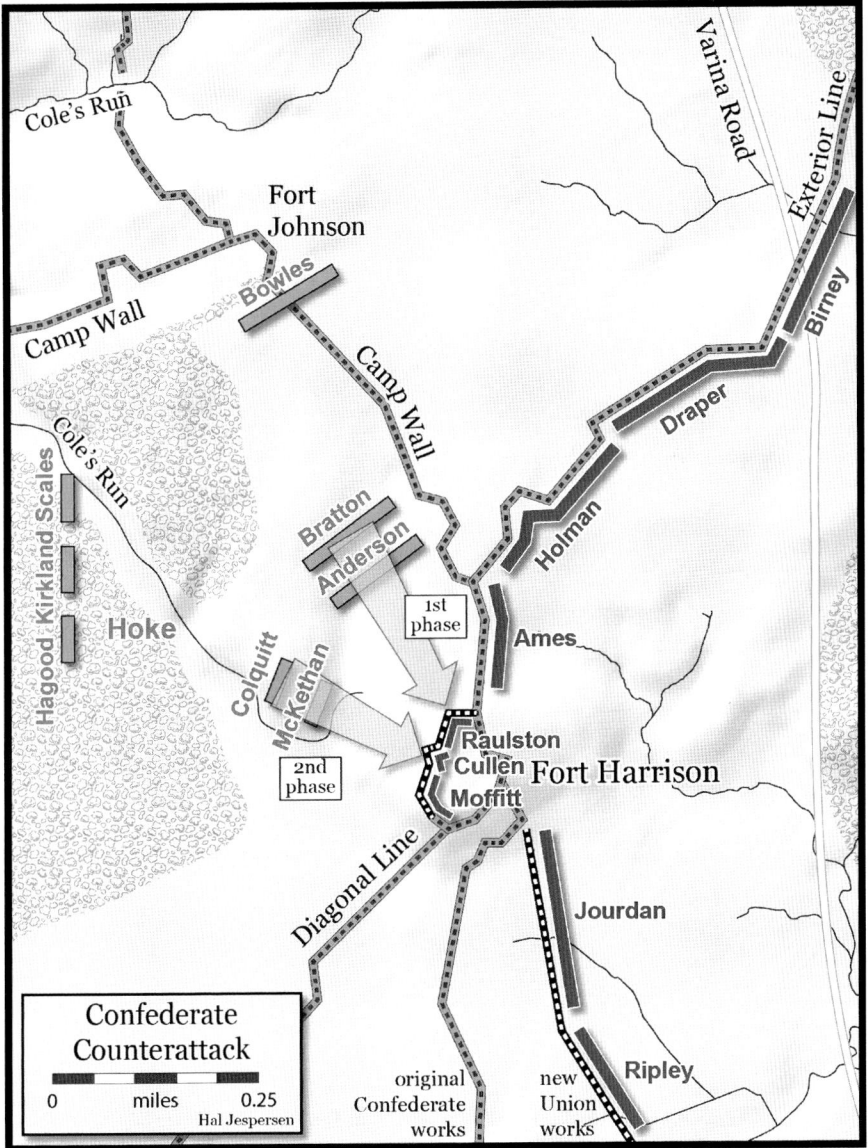

Confederate counterattack. Both "phases" were supposed to attack simultaneously. *Hal Jespersen.*

fort at the same time. G.T. Anderson's brigade, of Field's Division, was to advance "as close as possible to the work and let his men lay down, so as at the proper moment to spring up and reach the work simultaneously with Hoke." Bratton's brigade was to follow Anderson. At 1:45 p.m., Anderson was to step forward, and it was expected that he would be in place by 2:00 p.m., at which time the coordinated attack of Field and Hoke would commence.[228] The preliminary artillery barrage began after 11:00 a.m., when the three Confederate ironclads in the river opened fire, but their shooting was ineffective, and it was later stopped when Confederate officers warned that it threatened their own troops. Porter Alexander opened fire with his field artillery, but it, too, was not effective as it overshot its target when the gunners had difficulty seeing through the thick smoke.[229]

At 1:45 p.m., G.T. "Tige" Anderson's men stepped off, but the plan immediately began to go awry. Instead of advancing to the assigned point and lying down, Anderson's men "rushed forward to attack." Field was forced to respond by sending Bratton and then Bowles forward to assist. On the Confederate right, Hoke refused to move until the assigned hour, 2:00 p.m.[230]

Unfortunately for the Union troops, the attack was heading for the weakest part of the newly constructed rear wall at Fort Harrison. Not only that, but the little artillery that was available, part of the Third New York Artillery, was low on ammunition. Stannard called the failure of the unit's commanding officer to have his unit prepared and full of ammunition "reprehensible" and ordered the unit's cannon removed by hand, as horses could not be brought in. Stannard immediately dispatched a requisition to headquarters for a new battery and a "capable officer," but there was not enough time. The Georgians had begun the attack. The enemy would have to be repulsed by rifles and muskets alone.[231]

Anderson's men pressed directly on. A Confederate veteran remembered the charge: "The infantry moved forward at a double-quick, under the cover of the smoke which lay close to the ground in the heavy atmosphere. Nothing could be heard save the tramp of hurrying feet. Fort Harrison maintained an ominous silence." The attackers approached the fortifications and "suddenly...burst forth the famous rebel yell which fairly rent the air." All too soon, their worst fears were realized, as "there arose a long line of blue-clad soldiers, seemingly from out of the ground, who poured a deadly volley into the oncoming ranks."[232]

As the call arose along the Federal line—"They are forming!"—Stannard's men soon opened fire with their Spencer repeating rifles. A Union soldier recalled, "It was close range for the rifles of Stannard's Division and instantly there burst forth from those lines of breechloaders the most awful fire troops ever had to face. In our position on the left we could see nothing, while the roar of musketry was deep, unbroken and solid as the roar of Niagara."[233] H.E. Baker remembered the Confederate attack: "They formed for a charge in the lines of battle, and stared with a yell." He said the men handled the breechloaders "for all they were worth."[234] Another veteran said the attackers sounded like "an army of demons." When they were within range, there was an "unbroken blaze and crash of musketry, a solid volley." Each man took careful aim, and there was "not a random shot in the whole line." The attackers seemed "to wilt and sink down in the ground, as if it had suddenly opened beneath them."[235]

General Field was taken aback by Anderson's failure to lie down and ordered his other brigades to follow one hundred yards behind Anderson's, and "if they stopped to pass over them, and charge the enemy's works." The Confederates fought desperately. Field said that the Confederate dead lying "close under the enemy's works attest their honest efforts to achieve the object for which they were given." Soon his "shattered ranks were ordered to the rear to reform."[236] Advancing was difficult. Colonel Hagood of the First South Carolina, Bratton's Brigade, said, "At the critical moment the brigade which preceded us gave way, and rushing through our line caused immediate confusion."

As if there was not enough disorder, the huts that the Confederates had occupied as living quarters until the fall of the fort now provided some cover and "offered the temptation to skulk, which many failed to resist and which was impossible in the confusion to prevent." Hagood continued on "with those of my men who still adhered to their colors." His troops advanced until they were about sixty yards from the fort, then they could go no farther. "Here, owing to the little support which was accorded to me by the remainder of the brigade, I ordered a halt and began firing to divert my men." Failing to see reinforcements coming, the "enemy's fire impressed me with the necessity of falling back."[237]

The Federal defenders viewed the impressive display of the enemy advancing in "long lines of grey, and steadily, as if on a gala day parade," emerging "from the woods with flags flying, and the swords of his officers waving and flashing." Not to be outdone, bluecoats determined to make their stand. "Our flag is at once planted in the sand, unfurled, and all along our lines flag after flag is rapidly unfurled, until every bit of available color and bunting is set waving in the breeze as a challenge to the enemy to come on."[238]

As the Confederates advanced, Stannard climbed atop the high traverse and "paced up and down like an angry lion." The defenders would "rather face Lee's veterans in their fierce rage than the roar of that lion…the hearts of his men stopped beating as they saw his reckless daring." They knew what was at stake; the fate of the Army of the James depended on their ability to hold on.[239]

William Waud's wartime sketch of the Confederate counterattack. *LOC.*

A Union veteran remembered the ground trembling under the feet of the attackers. "They are within twenty rods of us now, marching and unbroken. A rider, a division commander, perhaps, dashes out before the second line formed of regiments in column and commands, high and loud, distinct and clear as a silver horn: 'Movement by battalion-deploy columns. By the right and left flanks. March!'" Although his action was brave, it was the officer's last. "That movement, in our front and under our fire, was fatal. That officer never saw his columns again. They collided, they recoiled, they fell, they fled."[240]

The battle became personal: Edwin Ware, first sergeant in Company G of the Thirteenth New Hampshire, looked to his right, toward a Confederate redoubt from which several shots had been fired at him. "Sergt. Albert M. Smith, Daniel W. Osborn and myself rested our gun on a little log in front of us, and when he raised his head again to fire, we fired simultaneously—and silenced his little battery."[241]

As in any battle, there were tales of individual heroism. Running low on ammunition and unable to get mule-drawn wagons into the area (Confederate sharpshooters picked off the mules), "Major Stoodley called for volunteers to go back for the boxes. Sergt. Gibbs [John F. Gibbs] started instantly and worked nobly lugging in the heavy boxes of ammunition in the face of heavy fire, for a considerable distance (over open ground) from the wagons to the battle lines. He deserved a promotion for it."[242] General Stannard wrote of the heroism of Captain John Brydon of the 118th New York and of two members of the general's staff: "It was in full view and but a short musket range from the enemy, yet Captain Brydon gallantly held his mules, three of which were shot while he was thus occupied, while Lieutenants Burbank and Cook, of my staff distributed the ammunition." Stannard said that the quick obedience to his orders and the "gallant manner" in which the men carried it out enabled his command to repulse the Confederate assaults."[213]

The Confederate plan was in shambles. What was originally planned as an assault by two of Field's brigades in conjunction with Hoke's had begun as a solo attack by Tige Anderson's brigade. In some ways, it was reminiscent of the Federal attacks of the previous day. The idea of massing force at one point was abandoned when Anderson's men failed to lie down and wait. Bratton was forced to follow, and when Anderson's men fell back, they disrupted Bratton's lines and helped to destroy any cohesion left in his attack. As it was not yet 2:00 p.m., the appointed hour, Hoke had not moved, and Federal fire could concentrate on Anderson and Bratton. The fire was intense. Lieutenant J.R.B. Best of the First South Carolina was wounded in the thigh and then in the chest. As he turned to go to the rear, he was hit in the back. Once on a stretcher, he was hit again and lost two toes. Amazingly, he survived.[214] George Benedict remembered a captured Confederate colonel looking up the traverse and yelling to Stannard, "Well, you had better get out of this, general, for General Lee is over there." Stannard's supposed reply was that he would be "happy to see General Lee whenever he chose to call."[215]

Four regiments of Bratton's Brigade managed to continue the fight and approached the fort. Stannard was resupplied with ammunition, and three guns from Battery K of the New York Light Artillery had arrived in the fort. The defenders blasted into Bratton's men. Most of the attackers held their ground or retreated, but Colonel James R. Hagood of the First South Carolina managed to reach within sixty yards of the fort. The Confederates retreated with losses of 30 percent.[216]

Although the Federal losses had been slight, one was of great significance. While leading the defense from the top of the Great Traverse, Stannard suddenly fell and "a shiver and whisper passed along the lines, as close as the cheers of victory came the whispered word 'Stannard is killed.'" However, that was not the case. Stannard was wounded in his right arm, which had to be amputated, ending his active service with the division. When his men learned that he had not been killed, "triumphant cheers rang out." Weitzel quickly acted and placed James Jourdan in command.[217]

Hoke had not advanced to aid Anderson and Bratton as planned because he had been ordered to move out at 2:00 p.m. and would not move a moment earlier. When he did attack, he left three brigades behind, some

4,200 men.[248] When Field saw this feeble effort, he decided not to join and attack again but rather took up a defensive position. The leading brigade would be Colonel Hector McKethan's (commanding in place of Clingman). The colonel had seen what had happened to Field's disjointed attack and knew that once they rose from the cover of the ridge, they would have to cross a killing field—several hundred yards of open ground—all the while facing the wrath of the Federal defenders who were positioned behind the improvised works, many armed with repeating rifles. Although he protested the assault as a terrible blunder, McKethan dutifully obeyed and led his men forward. Colquitt's Brigade was to follow. For whatever reason—whether he moved too fast and left Colquitt behind, or if Colquitt had held back—McKethan's Brigade outdistanced its support and advanced across the field. The full fury of the Federals was directed at them.

While the Federals' first volley fell short, the second hit its mark and tore into the North Carolinians. The Unionists' repeating rifles maximized the carnage. Brave souls kept moving forward, but they were immediately cut to pieces. Some of the men made it to the bottom of the fort's hill, but that was as far as they could advance under the hurricane of lead.[249] They hugged the ground at the base of the hill, fearing it was too dangerous to attempt to retreat. A sheet of flame met the advancing Confederates. It was as if "they dashed into the curvature of a sickle blade, and were cut down." Lieutenant R.B. Prescott of the Thirteenth New Hampshire said that they recognized a "certain Southern regiment" for which there was a bitter animosity, "on account of certain atrocities committed on our dead and wounded who had fallen into their hands." He expressed satisfaction that "most fearfully were those atrocities avenged." Clingman's Brigade (now under McKethan), to which this regiment belonged, was "practically annihilated."[250]

One of McKethan's men later wrote, "The time had arrived. The order was given to march…we had arrived at a place, down in a valley, at the bottom of a hill where the Battery was. Gels. Lee and Hoke stood upon an eminence in our rear." There they would "watch the charges and give us the signal." When the signal was given, "the command to charge was given to us by Col. McKetham [sic] who was in command of the brigade…I never saw men charge better in my life." They mounted the ridge and "as soon as we got upon the brow of it we charged toward the Fort. But our progress was stopped by stones and bryers [sic] which we had to charge over and through, under one of the severest cannonading and rifles shooting from thousands of rifles, for the Yankees were in there as thick as blackberries." They suffered many casualties, but "there were few of us who got there. The

Yankees had complete control of us. There was no retreating nor support us and consequently we lost nearly all our Brigade."[251]

A captain of the Thirty-first North Carolina recalled, "I…found the Yankees had massed their troops in the works right in our front having virtually vacated their left and I suppose they were three lines deep behind their works and they were all armed with seven shooters and the fire was awful." The Confederates continued their advance toward the fort, with the Federal repeating fire taking a terrible toll. "By the time we got in about seventy yards of their works our line was entirely broken not from falling back but literally from the men being cut down by piles by the brigade's fire."[252]

Colquitt soon pressed forward, but not as far as McKethan, and his men, too, were cut down. In about an hour's time, the Confederate counterattack had failed. It had gained nothing, and at a terrible price. One regiment, the Eighth North Carolina, began the attack with 175 officers and men. When the attack was over, twenty-five remained. Its commander, Colonel McKethan, "as long as he lived never could speak of this day without quivering lips and moistened eye when he described the fearful slaughter of his men in so hopeless an undertaking."[253]

Roughly 1,200 Confederates, all nearly impossible to replace, had been killed, wounded or were taken prisoner. The Federals, who could replace their casualties, had lost only about 260 men.[254] The Confederates chose not to attack again. Losses were severe, and it did not seem that any more could be gained without sacrificing more men in vain. Skirmishers were sent out to provide cover for McKethan's troops so they could retire, but the Federals fired on any who tried to escape. The North Carolinians would have to wait for dark to make their way back to their lines.[255] Their escape was not to be uncontested. As rain showers began to fall and they day turned to twilight, Federal sharpshooters left the protection of the fort and captured a number of Confederates.[256]

General Lee took the failure to recapture Fort Harrison very hard. His army, once so brilliant in the attack, now floundered and was disjointed. Porter Alexander remarked that the General "was more worried about this failure than I have ever seen him under similar circumstances."[257] Moxley Sorrel remembered events of that evening:

> General Lee, when he liked, could sit down pretty hard on words not agreeable to him. An example was given that night. With his staff and several general officers he was at the Chaffin farmhouse on the James, reviewing the serious events of the day. General John C. Pemberton, after

the fall of Vicksburg, being without assignment, had assumed his rank of Lieutenant Colonel in the Regular Army, and as such was on engineer duty on the Richmond line of defenses. He was present and, speaking of Battery Harrison, said with something like superior confidence, "I presume, General, you will retake the fort, coute que coute." Lee's sad, steady eyes rested on that unfortunate officer as he slowly said: "General Pemberton, I made my effort this morning and failed, losing many men killed and wounded. I have another line provided for that point and shall have no more blood shed at the fort unless you can show me a practical plan of capture; perhaps you can. I shall be glad to have it."[258]

Late in the afternoon, it began to rain, and through the night both sides could hear the tormenting cries of the wounded. Confederate stretcher-bearers sallied out but could not reach their comrades who lay close to the Federal lines. Some Union soldiers went out to provide water, and later Federal troops went out to capture the Confederate attackers who were still alive.[259]

Sergeant Nathaniel McKown "saw a Confederate flag go down about forty rods from where we were." He went out and asked the pickets "to watch for me as I came back, for I needed that flag badly." Crawling through the dead and wounded, McKown recalled speaking with a wounded Confederate, who said, "I would get killed if [I] went for it, but I replied that wounded men had no fight in them." After locating the flag, he "rolled it up, and started toward our lines." He said "my friend, the Confederate, and two or three others who were wounded so badly but that they could crawl, followed me in order to put themselves under the care of our surgeon." The sergeant was awarded the Medal of Honor for his adventure.[260]

On the morning of October 1, it appeared that Lee might be preparing to attack once again. He called a council of war and ordered the four ironclads plus the *Drewry* to open fire on the Federal positions, and infantry units began to form for an attack. The attack never happened.[261] Perhaps owing to his army's performance and the cost of the previous day, Lee opted not to renew the assault.[262] The Union troops worked to strengthen their defenses; the Confederates built a new defensive line anchored at Forts Maury and Hoke. While the Confederates had not recaptured the fort and ground lost on the twenty-ninth, they had stopped the Union offensive north of the river. The Union attack that had started with so much promise had ended. However, a number of the attackers would be heard from again. On April 3, 1865, some of the units that had fought at Chaffin's Farm would be the first to enter a fallen Richmond.

Chapter 8

Epilogue

On October 1, as the Federal troops looked across the ground to the Confederate earthworks in the distance, it must have seemed that a great opportunity had been lost. The attack of the twenty-ninth had started so well, with Confederates retreating from New Market Heights and Fort Harrison falling early that morning. The Federals took and held Fort Harrison to be sure, but the Confederates, now reinforced, stood between them and the prize of Richmond. The door that had seemed open a short time ago was now slammed shut. How had this happened?

Butler's plan had appeared to be solid, and when combined with an attack by Meade south of Petersburg, logic dictated that one end of the Confederate line would give way. One fatal misstep may have occurred early, in the allocation of troops for the attack. Butler took the Third Division from Ord's Eighteenth Corps and sent it with David Birney against New Market Heights. This ensured overwhelming odds in that sector. However, would the presence of that division have enabled the Federals to overcome the Confederate defenses at Fort Johnson and then turn and take Fort Gilmer in the open rear? It would seem likely, as a significant body of fresh troops could have been available to exploit the fall of Fort Harrison. J.B. Polley of the Texas Brigade said that had Butler "moved forward early on the morning with his whole force, the city must inevitably have been lost."[263] Confederate veteran Marcus J. Wright said that the Federals "could, had they continued, have marched into Richmond." Porter Alexander took things even further and questioned Grant's overall plan. He later wrote that Richmond would have fallen had the Federals put their whole strength into the Fort Harrison attack. "But he [Grant] made the mistake of striking upon both flanks at the same time, & neither blow was heavy enough to accomplish any important result."[261] In retrospect, it would seem that the Federals had adequate forces for both operations.

The shortcomings of the commander of the Army of the James did not stop with planning. Even more serious was his lack of leadership in the field. While Butler spent time at the New Market front, he paid only a cursory visit to the crucial attack at the Confederate center, where the success or failure of his plan would be decided. When Ord went down with a wound, the issue was still in the air. While the Eighteenth Corps could certainly have used its Third Division, it desperately needed leadership. When the issue was in the balance, Butler was nowhere to be found, despite his pledge "to keep himself in communication with the corps commanders, so as to afford any direction, advice, or assistance that may be in his power."[265] This should be compared with General Lee's response. When one of his flanks was threatened and the defense of Richmond was in doubt, Lee hurried to the scene to take personal command. Butler was missing when the critical developments at Forts Harrison, Johnson and Gilmer were deciding the outcome of not only the attack but possibly the course of the war as well. While Butler might have been an excellent politician and a fair campaign planner, he was no military leader. The failures of the Army of the James to take advantage of its available superior numbers the previous May at Port Walthall and Drewry's Bluff were repeated at Chaffin's Farm. There, too, he was absent.

Butler was not the only Union commander to make mistakes. General Ord believed in "leading from the front," and his corps paid for this when he went down with his wound. The Eighteenth Corps had lost key, experienced officers early on the morning of the twenty-ninth. With the loss of these field commanders, Ord's leadership was desperately needed. He had not issued written orders, and when he went down with his wound, Ord passed command of the Eighteenth Corps to Charles Heckman, with disastrous results. If the latter was clear on Ord's instructions, as Ripley indicated, he failed to obey them and follow on Stannard's right and attack the east front of Fort Harrison. In his report of the battle, Ord said, "Had General Heckman obeyed my orders many valuable lives would have been saved, and his division, reaching the work after Stannard's had taken it, would have been available to have attacked the only other work which intervened between us and Richmond in the rear; but he went too far into the woods, got his brigades scattered, and when found was not available in the right place."[266]

Ord also allowed his corps to get bogged down at Chaffin's Farm. The attack orders said that he was to avoid this and move up the Varina Road to meet the Tenth Corps. In fairness to Ord, the disorganized state of his corps after the Fort Harrison attack may have temporarily precluded this. He also was concerned about the possibility that Lee would send reinforcements over the bridge near Chaffin's Bluff, and his orders had addressed that. In any case, his wounding, and the loss of leadership that resulted, ruined any chances the Eighteenth Corps had of moving up the Varina Road, joining up with David Birney's command and moving on Richmond.

Heckman continued to make mistakes. His troops were scattered as they advanced through the thickets along Varina Road. As mentioned, he attacked piecemeal, first with his attacks on Batteries 10 and 11 to the right of Fort Harrison. After the latter fort fell to Stannard's Division, Fort Johnson, lightly defended, stood in the way of taking Fort Gilmer and advancing on Richmond. Heckman again ordered fragmented attacks by small units, rather than assaulting with a concentrated force, as Stannard had done at Fort Harrison. As a result, Fort Johnson held, and the rear of Fort Gilmer was blocked, forcing the Federals to make costly flank and frontal attacks on it. Colonel Edward H. Ripley, commander of Heckman's Second Brigade, termed it a "fatal mistake."[267] Heckman then ordered Ripley to attack Fort Gilmer with only a few of Heckman's troops and no coordination with Birney's force. Ripley wisely halted this suicidal mission.

The Federals continued similar tactics when David Birney's corps attacked Fort Gilmer. Instead of having Foster's attack timed with the assault by William Birney's USCTs, the Unionists launched disjointed attacks, permitting the defenders the ability to concentrate on one attacking force at a time.

While much can be said of the Union failures, a great deal of credit has to be given to the spirited defenders. Overwhelmingly outnumbered, they were originally stationed at the far ends of the defensive line, complicating the situation. General Gregg, realizing the peril that losing Fort Harrison could mean, rushed his Texas troops from the left flank and arrived in time to help save Fort Gilmer. Although Fort Harrison was overwhelmed by Stannard's concentrated attack, the Confederates quickly regrouped and formed a new line with Forts Johnson and Gilmer as key bulwarks. At Fort Johnson, a small, determined force held out against Heckman's mismanaged effort. At Fort Gilmer, they also held out as Federal attacks were repulsed and reinforcements began to arrive.

On September 29, General Ewell had one of his best days as a field commander. Showing signs of the form he once displayed when fighting under Stonewall Jackson, Ewell rose to the occasion and, in an extremely challenging situation, held off the Union attackers until help could arrive. A small number of veteran troops, buffered by a local defense force of all manner of men, had held out against a force of trained troops that vastly outnumbered them. For the Confederate defenders, it was a desperate but heroic day.

However, all things did not go the Confederates' way. On the thirtieth, their attack, designed by General Lee, was not carried out as planned. Coming from two different directions over varying terrain and distances, the two wings did not converge and attack the Federals simultaneously. Anderson's men, coming from the Federal right, failed to lie down and wait for the other troops to align. Possibly the fact that they were attacking over open ground, with the full attention of the Union defenders bearing down on them, caused them to attack prematurely. It is easy for the reader to sit back and find fault with their behavior, but reading a book is not the same as facing a shower of death being rained down on you. To truly understand a battle, one must walk the ground, seeing the undulations that might offer cover to some and the open ground that offers none. As you approach the defending earthworks, you can get a sense of the fear that might have gripped these troops. All of that being said, the failure of the Confederates to coordinate their drive doomed any chance the attack had of success. As had happened at Fort Gilmer, the defenders could focus their wrath on one segment of attackers at a time. Lee's army was also showing the effects of the losses suffered in leadership and veteran troops. It was no longer the army of the Peninsula, Second Manassas and Chancellorsville.

There would be further actions on Darbytown and Williamsburg Roads, but the main Union effort north of the river ended on September 30. While the Federals had secured a solid base north of the James River, they had failed to capitalize on one of the Union's best chances to capture Richmond. In a way, it was a tragedy for both sides. Many more men would die, and much suffering would be felt in both armies and on the homefront as the war dragged on. The war in Virginia would continue until the following spring. When the Confederates abandoned Richmond in April 1865 and lit fires, significant parts of Richmond burned. Some of the Federal troops who had been involved on September 29 and 30 would be among the first to enter the captured capital, and they would help to put those fires out.

Five years later, a reporter for the *Richmond Dispatch* visited Chaffin's Farm. "We saw in a small field north west of the fort…about fifty, or maybe more, bodies." As he continued to walk the ground he saw "four times that number in the nearby bushes." Perhaps the most sobering moment was when he saw that a farmer had "gathered up two piles of bones and burned them to ashes."[268] Whatever the successes and failures of the Fort Harrison campaign, it was indeed a human tragedy on so many levels.

Chapter 9

Fort Harrison Today

According to Dr. Louis Manarin, the "first battlefield tour" was held on Labor Day 1921, when Douglas Southall Freeman led a tour sponsored by the Richmond Rotary Club. A procession of twenty-one vehicles visited the unmarked battlefields, with Dr. Freemen interpreting. For a map, he used a bedsheet marked with liquid shoe polish. Confederate veterans from the Soldiers' Home were invited to join, and a number of them did. The Rotarians were inspired by the tour and saw the need to mark the sites and identify a tour route, so they appointed a commission, which would become the Battlefield Markers Association.[269]

The origins of the Richmond National Battlefield Park can be traced to the Battlefield Markers Association, formed in 1925 to finance, develop and install markers on key battlefield points in the Richmond area.[270] Noted historian Douglas Southall Freeman was the vice-president of this fledgling group. In 1927, learning that Fort Harrison was being sold, the group purchased two hundred acres, offsetting a portion of the roughly $4,000 price by selling the timber that had grown on the land.[271] Other battlefield sites were soon preserved, including land at Cold Harbor and Beaver Dam Creek. In 1928, sixty acres of the Gaines' Mill battlefield were purchased, as were one hundred acres at Malvern Hill. Additional land at Malvern Hill was later donated to the group.[272] In order to make the properties accessible, the Counties of Hanover, Henrico and Chesterfield chipped in and donated their entire 1929 gasoline tax revenues to the building of a state road through the properties.[273] In January 1932, the State of Virginia took over

A 1930s map showing the elevation of Fort Harrison, particularly from the east, south and west. *RNBP.*

the battlefields as its first state park, and 1936 saw the transfer of the park to the federal government.[271]

Today, impressive sets of fortifications remain well preserved at several of the parks, to the good fortune of posterity. In his history of the Richmond

Picture of the first park headquarters, now the visitor center at Fort Harrison. *RNBP.*

National Battlefield Park, historian John Willett stated, "After the war, many of the works on this part of the old Richmond front were so heavy that they did not repay the farmer for his labor in leveling them down, so they remained intact and undisturbed."[275] Over the years, the Richmond National Battlefield Park has gained additional land and thus has preserved more for future generations to see. The Civil War Trust and the Richmond Battlefields Association have purchased and preserved significant parcels of the area battlefields.

As the Great Depression raged in 1933, the Junior Colored Company 1375 of the Civilian Conservation Corps was assigned to the Richmond Battlefield Park to help develop Fort Harrison (as well as Forts Gilmer, Hoke and Cold Harbor). They laid out foot trails and cleared the fortifications. Fort Hoke was reconstructed from specifications found in wartime field manuals.[276] They also built a log cabin at Fort Harrison, which was to be used as a visitor center and park headquarters.[277] While the park later moved its headquarters to a building located on the site of the Chimborazo Hospital, it still uses the log cabin as a visitor center. What began with the purchase of some acreage of Fort Harrison would result in a large and complex national park, encompassing thirteen sites and all of the amazing stories behind them.

Fort Harrison appears quite different than it did in 1864. The fort sits on high ground, but this is disguised by the heavy growth to its front and rear. When the leaves are off the trees, one can see the rise leading to the east and south of the fort. To the rear (west), woods cover the approach of McKethan's men, but a short distance farther, one can see the ridge that had protected the Confederates before their September 30 attack. The park owns a narrow band of property that runs to Fort Johnson. Dwellings currently

CCC workers at Fort Harrison in 1938. *RNBP.*

Visitors at Fort Harrison in 1938. *RNBP.*

sit on much of the property surrounding that fort, but one can see the path Field's Confederates took in their attack from that direction.

Fort Gilmer still stands, and some of the ground over which Foster's men marched can still be seen. The ravines over which they traversed remain, although they have likely been partially filled in with the passing of time. The approach of the Fifth USCTs is all but gone. Tragically, the ground over which William Birney's USCTs advanced has been lost to a housing development, which extends all the way to the ditch at Fort Gilmer.

Through the efforts of many, the key forts and some of the ground involved in the fight can still be seen. With a little imagination, one can visit the area and understand the events of September 29 and 30, 1864. Today, the grounds are eerily quiet, but the earthworks that remain call out the savage fighting that occurred in their shadows. Many a man drew his last breath here.

Appendix I

The Leaders

Union[278]

David Bell Birney

Born in Huntsville, Alabama, in 1825, Birney moved to Ohio in 1838. He became an attorney and moved to Michigan and later to Pennsylvania. In April 1861, he was the lieutenant colonel of the Twenty-third Pennsylvania Militia and by February 1862 had been promoted to brigadier general. He served under General Heintzelman's command and was court-martialed for disobedience but was acquitted. By May 1863, he was a major general and was wounded at Gettysburg on July 2. At Spotsylvania on May 12, he was wounded again, this time by a shell fragment. He served as commander of the Tenth Corps of the Army of the James beginning July 23, 1864. Birney died of typhoid fever and dysentery in Philadelphia on October 18, 1864. He is buried in Woodlands Cemetery in Philadelphia.

William Birney

Brother of David Birney, William was born in Huntsville, Alabama, in 1819. A graduate of Yale, he became a professor of English at Bourges College in France and was a writer and editor for the *Philadelphia Register*. He was also an attorney. Birney joined the army as captain of the First New Jersey Infantry in May 1861. Captured at Alexander's Bridge outside Richmond on June 27, 1862, he was exchanged in August of that year and was wounded in the hip and left foot in Fredericksburg on December 13. Birney was promoted to brigadier general in May 1863 but spent most of the next year as a recruiting and mustering officer. In May 1864, he was assigned to the Army of the James. In March 1865, he was promoted to brevet major general. Birney later wrote *James G. Birney and His Times.* He died in Forest Glen, Maryland, in 1907 and is interred at the Oak Hill Cemetery in Georgetown.

Hiram Burnham

Born in Narraguagus (Cherryfield), Maine, in 1814, Burnham was a coroner and a lumberman. In July 1861, he was the lieutenant colonel of the Sixth Maine Infantry and served with the Army of the Potomac until April 1864, when he was promoted to brigadier general in the Army of the James. Burnham was killed leading his brigade in the assault at Fort Harrison. In his honor, the Union troops renamed the captured work "Fort Burnham." He is interred in the Pine Grove Cemetery in Cherryfield, Maine.

Benjamin Franklin Butler

A native of New Hampshire, Butler was born in Deerfield in 1818 and moved to Massachusetts in 1838. A teacher and a lawyer, Butler made most of his connections as a Massachusetts legislator. He was named brigadier general of the Massachusetts Militia in April 1861. Butler held a number of posts but was most famous for being the controversial military governor of New Orleans in 1862. He was named the commander of the Army of the James, where he displayed more vision than military skill. After the war, Butler became the governor of Massachusetts and later was a candidate for the presidency for the Greenback Party. He wrote several books, including *Butler's Book* and *Private and Official Correspondence of Gen. Benjamin F. Butler.* He died in Washington, D.C., in 1893 and is buried in Hildreth Cemetery in Lowell, Massachusetts.

Rufus Daggett

From Berlin, New York, born 1837, Daggett was a tinsmith and hardware merchant. Daggett was first lieutenant of the Fourteenth New York Infantry in May 1861. He rose to the rank of colonel in August 1864 and was wounded in the assault on Fort Gilmer. He was brevetted brigadier general in January 1865. After the war, he was a hardware merchant and a postmaster. Daggett died in 1912 and is interred in the New Forest Cemetery in Utica, New York.

Michael Thomas Donohoe

Born in Lowell, Massachusetts, in 1838, Donohoe had been a textile worker and a store clerk. In August 1861, he was a captain in the Third New Hampshire Infantry and was promoted to colonel in September. He was wounded at Fort Harrison and in March 1865 was brevetted as a brigadier general. After the war, Donohoe was a railway clerk, postal inspector and the superintendent of the Rainsford Island Reformatory. He passed away in 1895 and is buried at Holyhood Cemetery in Brookline, Massachusetts.

Robert Sanford Foster

Born in Vernon, Indiana, in 1834, Foster was a tinner. A private in the Indiana Infantry at the outbreak of the war, Foster rose to the rank of colonel within a year. By June 1863, he was a brigadier general and was sent to the Army of the James in April 1864. At the time of the Battle of Fort Harrison, he was in command of the Second Division of the Tenth Corps. Foster was brevetted a major general in March 1865. He was on the military commission for the trial of the conspirators for the assassination of President Lincoln. Later he became a U.S. marshal. He died in Indianapolis in 1903 and is buried at the Crown Hill Cemetery in that city.

Charles Adam Heckman

From Easton, Pennsylvania, Heckman was born in 1822. He graduated from the Minerva Seminary in 1837, became a sergeant in the U.S. Volunteers and was discharged in 1848. He took a job as a conductor for the New

Jersey Central Railroad. In April 1861, Heckman was a captain in the First Pennsylvania Infantry and by February of the following year had been promoted to colonel of the Ninth New Jersey Infantry. He was wounded at New Bern, North Carolina, in March 1862 and again at Young's Crossroads in July of that year. In November, he was promoted to brigadier general and spent much of the next year and a half serving along the coast. In April 1864, Heckman was a brigade commander in the Army of the James. Wounded at Port Walthall on May 7, he was captured at Second Drewry's Bluff on May 16 and was exchanged on September 12. Following the war, he was a conductor and dispatcher for the New Jersey Central Railroad. He died in 1896 and is buried in Easton, Pennsylvania.

Edward Otho Cresap Ord

From Cumberland, Maryland, Ord was born in 1818. He moved to Washington, D.C., in 1819 and was a graduate of the United States Military Academy. By September 1861, Ord was a brigadier general in McCall's Division of the Army of the Potomac. Sent to Tennessee in June 1862, he was wounded in the ankle at Hatchie River, Mississippi, in October of that year. In July 1864, he was in command of the Eighteenth Corps of the Army of the James and was wounded in the thigh during the Fort Harrison action. Ord remained with the army until his retirement in 1881. He became a construction engineer for Mexican railroads and wrote several books. Ord died of yellow fever while in Havana in 1883 and is buried in Arlington National Cemetery.

Galusha Pennypacker

Pennypacker was born in Valley Forge, Pennsylvania, in 1844. A sergeant in April 1861, he rose to the rank of lieutenant colonel by April 1864. He was wounded in the right elbow, right shoulder and left knee in Green Plains, Virginia, in May 1864. In August 1864, he was promoted to colonel and was wounded in the right ankle in the attack on Fort Gilmer. The following January, he was wounded in the right side and hip at Fort Fisher, North Carolina, and was promoted to brigadier general in February at the age of twenty. In March, he was brevetted major general. For his actions at Fort Fisher, he was awarded the Medal of Honor in 1883. He retired as a brigadier general in the regular army in 1904 and passed away in 1916. His remains rest at the Philadelphia National Cemetery, Philadelphia.

Edward Hastings Ripley

From Rutland, Vermont, Ripley was born in 1839. In July 1862, he was a captain in the Ninth Vermont Infantry and was captured at Harpers Ferry in September of that year. Exchanged in January 1863, he rose through the ranks and was promoted to colonel in June of that year. Ripley was promoted to brevet brigadier general in August 1864 and was wounded during the action at Fort Harrison. After the war, he became a marble industry executive and wrote *The Capture and Occupation of Richmond, April 3rd, 1865*, and his experiences were described in *Vermont General: The Unusual War Experiences of Edward Hastings Ripley*. He died in 1915 and is buried in the Evergreen Cemetery in Rutland, Vermont.

Samuel Henry Roberts

Born in East Hartford, Connecticut, in 1820, Roberts had been a salesman and a bookkeeper before the war. In September 1862, he was a lieutenant colonel in the 139th New York Infantry. Roberts was named brevet brigadier general in the Eighteenth Corps for his work at Fort Harrison. Following the war, he was a clerk in the Brooklyn Navy Yard and died in 1890. He is interred in the Evergreen Cemetery in Brooklyn.

George Jerrison Stannard

A native of Georgia, Vermont, Stannard was born in 1820. He was a farmer, teacher and foundry clerk. In June 1861, Stannard was the lieutenant colonel of the Ninth Vermont Infantry and was captured at Harpers Ferry on September 15, 1862. Exchanged in January, he was promoted to brigadier general in March 1863. Stannard was wounded in the right thigh at Gettysburg on July 3 and in the left thigh at Cold Harbor. Later in June 1864, he was appointed a division commander in the Army of the James. Stannard was wounded in his left arm in Petersburg in July, and in September, he lost his right arm at Fort Harrison. In October, he was promoted to brevet major general. He was assigned to a commission to establish a hospital for wounded veterans and later was appointed superintendent of Freedmen's Affairs in Maryland. Stannard was the doorkeeper at the U.S. House of Representatives from 1881 to 1886. He died in Washington in 1886 and is buried in Lake View Cemetery in Burlington, Vermont.

Confederate

Frederick Samuel Bass

Bass was born in Brunswick County, Virginia, in 1829. He was a graduate of the Virginia Military Institute and was a teacher in Texas before the war. Bass was the captain of Company E, First Texas, in May 1861. He rose in rank and was promoted to colonel in July 1864. Bass was wounded in action on Darbytown Road on October 7, 1864. He was among those paroled at Appomattox. Bass became the president of Marshall University in Texas. He died in Austin, Texas, in 1897 and is buried in the state cemetery there.[279]

Dudley McIvor DuBose

Born in 1834 in Shelby County, Tennessee, DuBose attended the University of Mississippi and the Lebanon Law School. He moved to Georgia, where he married the daughter of United States senator Robert Toombs. At the outbreak of hostilities, he was appointed a lieutenant in the Fifteenth Georgia but eventually joined Toombs's staff. In 1863, he became a colonel of the Fifteenth Georgia and participated in the Suffolk and Gettysburg campaigns. He fought at Chickamauga, where he was wounded; participated in actions at Chattanooga and Knoxville, the Wilderness, Spotsylvania and Cold Harbor; and was a brigade commander in the Chaffin's Farm area in September 1864. He was promoted to brigadier general in December 1864 and was captured at Sailor's Creek on April 6. After the war, DuBose opened a law office in Washington, Georgia, and served one term in the U.S. House of Representatives. He passed away in 1883 and is interred in Rest Haven Cemetery in Washington, Georgia.[280]

Richard Stoddert Ewell

Born in 1817, Ewell was from Georgetown in the District of Columbia. His grandfather had been a colonel during the American Revolution, but Richard lived in poverty. Without the means to attend college, he was fortunate to be appointed to the United States Military Academy. Ewell fought in the Mexican War, where he was brevetted captain for his brave service, and participated in military expeditions on the American western frontier. When Virginia seceded, Ewell resigned his commission and was named a lieutenant colonel of cavalry. Soon thereafter, he was promoted to brigadier general and took part in the First Battle of Manassas. In January 1862, he was promoted to major general and served in the valley under Jackson. Ewell fought in the Seven Days, at Cedar Mountain and at Groveton, where a wound necessitated the amputation of his leg. He returned to action in time for the Gettysburg campaign and was named corps commander when the army was reorganized after Jackson's death at Chancellorsville. Lee was not entirely satisfied with Ewell's performance in this role and ordered him to the Department of Richmond in 1864. He gallantly led the defense at Chaffin's Farm. On April 6, 1865, he was captured at Sailor's Creek. After the war, he operated his wife's plantation in Tennessee and died there in 1872. He is buried in the Old City Cemetery in Nashville.[281]

Charles William Field

A Kentuckian, Field was born in 1828 and attended the United States Military Academy, graduating in 1849. When Virginia and the other border states seceded, Field resigned his commission in the U.S. Army and was named the colonel of the Sixth Virginia Cavalry. In March 1862, he was appointed brigadier general. His first real action was at Beaver Dam Creek and throughout the Seven Days campaign, and he took part in the action at Cedar Mountain and at Second Manassas, where he received a serious wound. While recuperating, he served with Richmond's Bureau of Conscription, and once he was able to return to active service, he was promoted to major general. He was assigned command of Hood's Division, while that commander recovered from the loss of a leg at Chickamauga. Field saw action at the Wilderness and was riding with Longstreet when the latter and Micah Jenkins were hit by friendly fire. He fought with his unit in all of its actions to Appomattox. After the war, he held a variety of positions, including executive with a life insurance company, officer in the army of the Khedive of Egypt, door keeper at the House of Representatives, civil engineer and manager of an Indian reservation. He died in 1892 and is buried in Loudon Park Cemetery in Baltimore.[282]

John Gregg

Born in 1828, Gregg was from Lawrence County, Alabama. He studied and practiced law in Texas and won a district judgeship when he was twenty-eight. In 1861, Gregg was chosen to be a delegate to the state convention called to vote on secession. He was elected a Texas representative to the new Confederate government in Montgomery, Alabama, and thence moved with it to Richmond. He gave up his seat in July 1861 to organize the Seventh Texas and was elected its colonel. Gregg was taken prisoner at Fort Donelson and released several months later. He was active in several western campaigns and was wounded at Chickamauga. He fought in the Wilderness and in all the actions of the First Corps until he was shot and killed outside Richmond on October 7, 1864.[283]

Richard Cornelius Taylor

Born in Norfolk, Virginia, in 1835, Taylor attended the Virginia Military Academy and became a railroad auditor. In April 1861, he was captain of Company H of the Sixth Virginia. In March 1862, Taylor was a major of artillery and then held several staff functions. He was in command at Fort Harrison on September 29, where he was wounded twice and taken prisoner. Following the war, he was a teacher in Norfolk. Taylor died in 1917 and is buried in the Elmwood Cemetery there. He was the brother of staff officer W.H. Taylor.[284]

Appendix II

Order of Battle

UNION: ARMY OF THE JAMES
Major General Benjamin F. Butler

XVIII Corps
Major General Edward O.C. Ord

First Division
Brigadier General George J. Stannard

First Brigade
Colonel Aaron F. Stevens
13th New Hampshire
81st New York
98th New York
139th New York

Second Brigade
Brigadier General Hiram Burnham
8th Connecticut
10th New Hampshire

Second Division
Brigadier General Charles
A. Heckman

First Brigade
Colonel James Jourdan
148th New York
158th New York
55th Pennsylvania

Second Brigade
Colonel Edward H. Ripley
8th Maine
9th Vermont

96th New York
118th New York

Third Brigade
Colonel Samuel H. Roberts
21st Connecticut
92nd New York
58th Pennsylvania
188th Pennsylvania

Third Brigade
Colonel Harrison S. Fairchild
89th New York
2d Pennsylvania Heavy Artillery

Third Division (attached to X Corps for Chaffin's Farm/New Market Heights
    Campaign)
Brigadier General Charles J. Paine

First Brigade
Colonel John H. Holman
1st U.S. Colored Troops (USCTs)
22nd USCTs
37th USCTs

Second Brigade
Colonel Alonzo G. Draper
5th USCTs
36th USCTs
38th USCTs

Third Brigade
Colonel Samuel A. Duncan
4th USCTs
6th USCTs
10th USCTs

Unattached
2nd USCT Cavalry

Artillery
Major General George B. Cook
3rd New York Light, Batteries E, H, K, M

New York Light, 7th Battery
New York Light, 16th Battery
New York Light, 17th Battery
1st Pennsylvania Light, Battery A
1st Rhode Island Light, Battery F
1st United States, Battery B (*listed in O.R., not listed by Sommers*)
4th United States, Battery L
5th United States, Batteries A, F

X Corps
Major General David B. Birney

First Division	*Second Division*
Brevet Major General Alfred H. Terry	Brigadier General Robert S. Foster
First Brigade	*First Brigade*
Colonel Francis B. Pond	Colonel Rufus Daggett
39th Illinois	3rd New York
62nd Ohio	12th New York
67th Ohio	117th New York
85th Pennsylvania	142nd New York
Second Brigade	*Second Brigade*
Colonel Joseph C. Abbott	Colonel Galusha Pennypacker
6th Connecticut	47th New York
7th Connecticut	48th New York
3rd New Hampshire	76th Pennsylvania
7th New Hampshire	97th Pennsylvania
16th New York Heavy Artillery	203rd Pennsylvania
Third Brigade	*Third Brigade*
Colonel Harris M. Plaisted	Colonel Louis Bell
10th Connecticut	13th Indiana
11th Maine	9th Maine
1st Maryland Cavalry (dismounted)	4th New Hampshire
24th Massachusetts	115th New York
100th New York	169th New York

Colored Brigade
Brigadier General William Birney
29th Connecticut
7th USCTs
8th USCTs
9th USCTs
45th USCTs

Artillery
Lt. Colonel Richard H. Jackson
Connecticut Light, 1st Battery
New Jersey Light, Batteries 4, 5
Section of 16th New York Heavy Artillery
1st Pennsylvania Light, Battery E
3rd Rhode Island Light, Battery C
1st United States, Batteries C, D, M
3rd United States, Battery E
4th United States, Battery D

Temporary Brigade
Maj. David B. White
5th Maryland
2nd New Hampshire
12th New Hampshire

Provisional Brigade
Colonel Joseph Potter
11th Connecticut
40th Massachusetts
200th Pennsylvania
205th Pennsylvania
206th Pennsylvania
207th Pennsylvania
208th Pennsylvania
209th Pennsylvania
211th Pennsylvania

CONFEDERATE
Lieutenant General Richard Ewell—Brigadier General John Gregg

Major General Robert Hoke's Division

Clingman's Brigade (Colonel Hector McKethan)
8th North Carolina
31st North Carolina
51st North Carolina
61st North Carolina

Brigadier Gen. Johnson Hagood
7th South Carolina Battalion
11th South Carolina
21st South Carolina
25th South Carolina
27th South Carolina

Brigadier General Alfred Colquitt
6th Georgia
19th Georgia
23rd Georgia
27th Georgia
28th Georgia

Brigadier Gen William Kirkland
17th North Carolina
42nd North Carolina
66th North Carolina

Major General Charles Field's Division

Brigadier General John Bratton
1st South Carolina
2nd South Carolina Rifles
5th South Carolina
6th South Carolina
Palmetto Sharpshooters

Brigadier Gen. George Anderson
7th Georgia
8th Georgia
9th Georgia
11th Georgia
59th Georgia

Benning's Brigade (Colonel Dudley DuBose)
2nd Georgia
15th Georgia
17th Georgia
20th Georgia

Gregg's Brigade (Col. Fred. Bass)
1st Texas
4th Texas
5th Texas
3rd Arkansas

Law's Brigade (Brigadier General Pinckney Bowles)
4th Alabama
15th Alabama
44th Alabama

47th Alabama
48th Alabama

Johnson's Brigade (Colonel John Hughs)
17th Tennessee
23rd Tennessee
25th Tennessee
44th Tennessee
63rd Tennessee

Colonel Alfred Scales (from Wilcox's Division)
13th North Carolina
16th North Carolina
22nd North Carolina
34th North Carolina
38th North Carolina

Brigadier General Martin Gary's Cavalry
7th South Carolina Cavalry
24th Virginia Cavalry
Hampton's Legion

From Pickett's Division (Colonel Edgar Montague)
24th Virginia
32nd Virginia
53rd Virginia
56th Virginia

Local Defense Troops
1st Regiment Virginia Reserves
1st Battalion, Virginia Reserves
2nd Battalion, Virginia Reserves
3rd Battalion, Virginia Reserves
4th Battalion, Virginia Reserves
5th Battalion, Virginia Reserves
25th Virginia Battalion (Manarin, 2:576, 601)

Militia
Virginia City Battalion (Manarin, 2:568)
1st City Regiment
2nd City Regiment
3rd City Regiment
4th City Regiment
Castle Thunder Company

Maury's Artillery (Taylor)
Lunenburg Artillery
Goochland Artillery
Pamunkey Artillery
Halifax Light Artillery
James City Artillery

Hardaway's Battalion, 1st Corps Artillery
1st Rockbridge Artillery
1st Virginia Light
3rd Richmond Howitzers
Powhatan Artillery
Salem Flying Artillery

Haskell's Battalion, 1st Corps Artillery
Branch's N.C. Battery
Rowan, N.C. Battery
Palmetto Artillery
Nelson, Va. Battery

Giles Virginia Light Artillery
Louisiana Guard Artillery
McIntosh's Battalion, 3rd Corps Artillery
Mathews (Va.) Artillery
Fredericksburg Artillery
Jackson Flying Artillery

The Order of Battle is taken from Sommers, Richmond Redeemed, *459–71 and*
O.R., *series 1, volume 42, part 1, 133–38. If so noted, some references are to Manarin,*
vol. 2.

Notes

Abbreviations for cited sources:
HC: Henrico County
LOC: Library of Congress
MHRC: U.S. Army Military History Institute
OR: U.S. War Department, *War of the Rebellion*. All citations are to series 1, with the volume and part listed individually.
RNBP: Richmond National Battlefield Park

PROLOGUE

1. Rick Atkinson, *An Army At Dawn: The War in North Africa, 1942–1943* (New York: Henry Holt and Company, 2002).

CHAPTER 1

2. Grant, *Memoirs*, 412.
3. Dowdey, *Lee's Last Campaign*, 55.
4. Rhea, *Battle of the Wilderness*, 21. Anyone with an interest in the Overland Campaign, as the 1864 drive by Grant is known, would profit from reading Rhea's series of books. Thoroughly researched and well written, they are currently considered to be some of the finest works on the subject.
5. Ibid., 435, 440.
6. Grant, *Memoirs*, 473; *OR*, vol. 36, part 2, Grant to Halleck, May 11, 1864, 627–28.

7. Rhea, *Spotsylvania*, 312.
8. Grant, *Memoirs*, 503.
9. Rhea, *Cold Harbor, Grant and Lee May 26–June 3, 1864*, 393. Estimates on the losses from May 5 through June 12 vary, but Rhea's work is based on thorough research and also is close to the estimate provided by Confederate general Edward Porter Alexander in his personal memoirs, *Fighting for the Confederacy*, 434. Grant estimated his losses at 39,529 in his *Memoirs*, 513.
10. *OR*, vol. 42, part 2, Lincoln to Grant, September 29, 9:40 a.m., 1090.
11. Grant, *Memoirs*, 505–6.
12. *OR*, vol. 40, part 1, 17, quoted in McPherson, *Battle Cry of Freedom*, 760.
13. McPherson, *Battle Cry of Freedom*, 780.
14. *OR*, vol. 42, part 2, Lee to the Secretary of War, 1194.
15. Ibid., 1200.
16. Robertson, *Back Door to Richmond*, 16–22.
17. Ibid., 89.
18. *OR*, vol. 46, part 1, Grant's Report of July 22, 1865, 19.

CHAPTER 2

19. Jones, *Generals*, 1:61.
20. Butler, *Correspondence of Gen. Benjamin F. Butler*, 1:185–88.
21. Price, *Battle of New Market Heights*, 29.
22. Jones, *Generals*, 64.
23. Ibid., 65.
24. McPherson, *Tried by War*, 222–23.
25. Van Lew, *Yankee Spy in Richmond*, from the introduction by editor David D. Ryan, 8.
26. Manarin, *Henrico County Fields of Honor*, 2:569.
27. Sommers, *Richmond Redeemed*, 3–4; Grant, *Memoirs*, 546.
28. These actions are referred to as the "First " and "Second" Deep Bottom Campaigns. For more information, see Sommers, *Richmond Redeemed*; Manarin, *Henrico County*, vol. 2.
29. Several period maps of the Richmond fortifications are available. Jedediah Hotchkiss's map is available at the Library of Congress catalogue, as is the map discovered on the body of Confederate general John Chambliss. The U.S. Army Corps of Engineers developed maps, known as the Michler and Michie Maps, which can be found in the Official Records Atlas. Also in those records is the map by Confederate captain A.H. Campbell.
30. Manarin, *Henrico County*, 2:568; *OR*, vol. 42, part 2, Brigadier General C.J. Paine to General Butler's Chief of Staff, 766.

31. Sommers, *Richmond Redeemed*, 17.
32. *OR*, vol. 42, part 2, Butler's Orders, September 29, 1864, 1083–84.
33. Pfanz, *Richard S. Ewell*, 412; Alexander, *Fighting for the Confederacy*, 475.
34. *OR*, vol. 42, part 2, Ewell's return of September 20, 1864, 1266.
35. Sommers, *Richmond Redeemed*, 5. Later in his work (27, 28), Sommers states that the Tenth Corps might have had as few as 10,300 men, plus Paine's 3,800 from the Eighteenth Corps, giving him a total of 14,100 effectives. With roughly 8,000 traveling with Ord, Butler may have only had a bit over 22,000 men going to the north side.
36. Price, *Battle of New Market Heights*, 22–23.
37. Sommers, *Richmond Redeemed*, 17.
38. *OR*, vol. 42, part 2, Walter Taylor to Lieutenant General R.H. Anderson. September 23, 1864, 1298.
39. Ibid., 18.
40. Sommers, "Grant's Fifth Offensive," 30, 55; Sommers, *Richmond Redeemed*, 5.
41. *OR*, vol. 42, part 2, Grant to Meade, September 25, 7:00 p.m., 1010.
42. Ibid., Grant to Meade, 1046–47.
43. Ibid., Grant to Butler, 1058–59.
44. Sommers, *Richmond Redeemed*, 18–19.
45. *OR*, vol. 42, part 2, Butler to Ord, Sept 28, 1084–86.
46. Ibid., 1088.
47. Davis, *Death in the Trenches*, 139; Sommers, *Richmond Redeemed*, 23.
48. Trudeau, *The Last Citadel*, 208.

CHAPTER 3

49. Warner, *Generals in Blue*; 471; Eicher and Eicher, *Civil War High Command*, 505; Dickson, "Second Vermont Biographies/Obituaries." Based on a report by Dr. Leroy M. Bingham in pension file.
50. Zeller, *Ninth Vermont Infantry*, 165; Eicher and Eicher, *Civil War High Command*, 292, quote attributed to Colonel Ripley.
51. Zeller, *Ninth Vermont Infantry*, 164; Eicher and Eicher, *Civil War High Command*, 292.
52. *OR*, vol. 42, part 1, Ord's Report of June 15, 1865, 793; Humphreys, *Virginia Campaign*, 285; Thompson, *Thirteenth Regiment*, 459; Manarin, *Henrico County*, 2:582; Sommers, *Civil War Times Illustrated* 19, no. 6 (October 1980); Sommers, *Richmond Redeemed*, 42; Zeller, *Ninth Vermont Infantry*, 164; Sommers, "Grant's Fifth Offensive," 183–84. Although one would assume the commander's figures were reliable, Sommers makes a strong argument that in this case, Ord had unintentionally

underestimated his command by not counting all of the troops in Heckman's division. According to Sommers, Stannard claimed to have 2,855 men in his division alone (in his April 18, 1865 report). To this, one would have to add Heckman's division of approximately 4,095. Added to this would be the engineers and others for a total of 8,135 effectives.

53. *OR*, vol. 42, part 1, 793.
54. Dickinson, *Engineering Operations at Chaffin's Bluff*, 7, 15.
55. Sommers, *Civil War Times Illustrated* (October 1980): 17–18; Dickinson, *Engineering Operations at Chaffin's Farm*, 21.
56. Sommers, *Richmond Redeemed*, 42.
57. Sommers, *CWTI* (October 1980): 19. It should be noted that the exact number of guns in the fort is still disputed.
58. Manarin, *Henrico County*, 2:603–5.
59. Moore, "The Attack of Fort Harrison," 418.
60. Manarin, *Henrico County*, 2:601.
61. Krick, *Staff Officers in Gray*, 282–83.
62. Prescott, *Capture of Richmond*.
63. *OR*, vol. 42, part 1, Stannard's Report, April 18, 1865, 798; Ripley, "First Hand Account of Battle of Fort Harrison," *Richmond News Leader*, April 27, 1939.
64. Sommers, *Richmond Redeemed*, 26.
65. *OR*, vol. 42, part 1, Stannard's Report, 798.
66. Prescott, *Capture of Richmond*.
67. *OR*, vol. 42, part 1, Peter S. Michie Report, October 10, 1864, 662.
68. "Personal Experience of Major Richard C. Taylor, Confederate Army," cited in Calrow, 27.
69. Sommers, *Richmond Redeemed*, 28; Manarin, *Henrico County*, 2:602; *OR*, vol. 42, part 2, order from Jno. Withers, Assistant Adjutant-General, 1301.
70. "Personal Experience of Major Richard C. Taylor, Confederate Army," cited in Calrow, "Battle of Chaffin's Farm," 27.
71. Sommers, *Richmond Redeemed*, 41–42; Manarin, *Henrico County*, 2:602–3.
72. *OR*, vol. 42, part 1, Ord's Report of June 15, 1865, 793–94.
73. Thompson, *Thirteenth Regiment*, 460–61.
74. Warner, *Generals in Blue*, 55–56; Eicher and Eicher, *Civil War High Command*, 155; Rhea, *Cold Harbor*, 228.
75. Sommers, *Richmond Redeemed*, 44; Thompson, *Thirteenth Regiment*, 478.
76. Thompson, *Thirteenth Regiment*, 460.
77. Breckenridge, "Story of a Boy Captain," 415.
78. Prescott, *Capture of Richmond*.
79. Manarin, *Henrico County*, 2:605.
80. Thompson, *Thirteenth Regiment*, 461.
81. Ibid., 488.

82. *OR*, vol. 42, part 1, Stannard's Report, 798.

83. Sommers, *Richmond Redeemed*, 46.

84. Thompson, *Thirteenth Regiment*, 461.

85. Prescott, *Capture of Richmond*.

86. Taylor, "Personal Experience," quoted in Calrow, "Battle of Chaffin's Farm," 27.

87. Sommers, *Richmond Redeemed*, 46.

88. Ware, "Battery Harrison."

89. Polley, *A Soldier's Letters*, 165.

90. Moore, "The Attack of Fort Harrison."

Chapter 4

91. Thompson, *Thirteenth Regiment*, 478–79.

92. Ibid., 462.

93. Prescott, *Capture of Richmond*.

94. Baker, "In Front of Richmond."

95. Thompson, *Thirteenth Regiment*, 471.

96. Prescott, *Capture of Richmond*.

97. *OR*, vol. 42, part 1, Major Normand Smith's, Report of October 22, 1864, 805.

98. Moore, "The Attack on Fort Harrison," 419; Manarin, *Henrico County*, 2:615.

99. Beyer & Keydel, *Deeds of Valor*, 432.

100. "Personal Experience of Major Richard C. Taylor," quoted in Calrow, 27.

101. Beyer and Keydel, *Deeds of Valor*, 432–33; Cecil Clay letter to the *National Tribune*, May 2, 1889.

102. Wallace, *Story of American Heroism*.

103. *Delaware County Republican*, October 14, 1864.

104. Sommers, *Richmond Redeemed*, 47–48.

105. Thompson, *Thirteenth Regiment*, 462.

106. Moore, "The Attack of Fort Harrison," 419.

107. *OR*, vol. 42, part 1, Stannard's Report, April 18, 1865, 799.

108. *OR*, vol. 42, part 1, Ord's Report of June 15, 1865, 794.

109. Ibid., 793. Ord stated that to provide greater secrecy, he did not give orders, so complete proof that Heckman was aware of these orders is not available. However, it is most probable that Ord verbally gave him these instructions, as they make sense in terms of Ord's overall plan of attack. Additionally, Heckman's subordinate, Ripley, corroborated Ord's report.

110. Ripley, "First Hand Account"; Zeller, *Ninth Vermont*, 173.

111. Sommers, *Richmond Redeemed*, 54.

112. Ibid., 52. In regard to the curtain of trees just south of Fort Johnson, it had previously been this author's opinion that the land was bare and open between the two forts. Photographs from 1865 and beyond show open fields around Fort Johnson. Historian Mike Gorman, of the Richmond National Battlefield Park, quite well known for his work with Civil War photography, made an interesting discovery. He studied a post-battle picture facing in the direction of the new Confederate line at Fort Beauregard. On top of this he superimposed a modern aerial map. With the modern roads visible, he could trace the line of the Confederate counterattack from the Fort Johnson area. The line of trees was clearly in the path between the two forts. See the picture on page 80. To the right side of the photograph, the line of trees can be seen. Additionally, H.E. Baker, in the *Adirondack Record* of July 25, 1919, mentions that on the thirtieth, the Confederates, retreating toward Fort Johnson, were "sheltered by some timbers that stood between the two lines." Pictures taken in later years do not show the line of trees, which can be expected, as soldiers likely would have cut them down to use as firewood during their winter encampments in the area.

113. Ibid., 54–55; Ripley, "First Hand Account."

114. Ibid.; Benedict, *Vermont in the Civil War,* 2:241; Manarin, *Henrico County,* 2:617.

115. Ripley, "First Hand Account."

116. Sommers, *Richmond Redeemed,* 55.

117. Manarin, *Henrico County,* 2:617; Sommers, *Richmond Redeemed,* 55–57; Zeller, *Ninth Vermont,* 167–71.

118. Ripley, "First Hand Account"; Benedict, *Vermont in the Civil War,* 242.

119. Manarin, *Henrico County,* 2:617–18; Sommers, *Richmond Redeemed,* 57.

120. Manarin, *Henrico County,* 2:618.

121. Dowdey and Manarin, *The Wartime Papers of Robert E. Lee,* 859–60; *OR,* vol. 42, part 2, Lee to Bragg, 1302, Lee to Ewell, 1304.

122. *OR,* vol. 42, part 2, Walter Taylor to John Gregg, September 29, 1864, 1305.

123. Pfanz, *Richard S. Ewell,* 417.

124. Jones, *Rebel War Clerk's Diary,* 427.

125. Ibid., 416; Sommers, "Grant's Fifth Offensive," 227–28; Sommers, *Richmond Redeemed,* 28, 51, 62–63.

126. Charles Johnson, "Fort Gilmer," quoted in Pfanz, Richard Stoddert Ewell Letterbook, Manuscript Department, William R. Perkins Library, Duke University, Durham, NC, 439–40.

127. Sommers, "Grant's Fifth Offensive," 1:228; Pfanz, *Richard S. Ewell,* 417.

CHAPTER 5

128. *OR*, vol. 42, part 1, Ord's Report of June 15, 1865, 794.

129. *OR*, vol. 42, part 1, Butler's Orders of September 28, 1085.

130. Manarin, *Henrico County*, 2:627–28.

131. Sommers, *Richmond Redeemed*, 59–60.

132. Manarin, *Henrico County*, 629; Sommers, *Richmond Redeemed*, 60–61; Allen, "Fight at Chaffin's Farm," 418.

133. *OR*, Navy, vol. 10, Report of Commander Thomas R. Rootes, October 4, 1864, 762.

134. Manarin, *Henrico County*, 2:630–31; Sommers, *Richmond Redeemed*, 72–73; Coski, *Capital Navy*, 167–68; *Official Records of the Union and Confederate Navies*, 753–62.

135. *OR*, vol. 42, part 1, Ord's Report, 794.

136. Manarin, *Henrico County*, 2:629–31; *OR*, vol. 42, part 1, Stannard's Report of April 18, 1865, 799.

137. *OR*, vol. 42, part 1, Stannard's Report, 799. In his report Stannard recommended that both officers receive promotions for their "highly meritorious conduct."

138. *OR*, vol. 42, part 1, Ord's Report, 794; Sommers, *Richmond Redeemed*, 64.

139. Benedict, *Vermont in the Civil War*, 2:243.

140. Zeller, *Ninth Vermont Infantry*, 172–76.

141. Ibid., 177–78.

142. Ibid., 177; Ripley, "First Hand Account."

143. Allen, "Fight at Chaffin's Farm," 418.

144. Sommers, *Richmond Redeemed*, 65–67.

145. J.M. Alexander, "Army of the James," *National Tribune*, July 30, 1890.

146. Manarin, *Henrico County*, 2:632–37; Sommers, *Richmond Redeemed*, 66–69.

147. Sommers, *Richmond Redeemed*, 74–77; *OR*, vol. 42, part 1, Ord's Report, 795; Ripley, "First Hand Account."

148. Thompson, *Thirteenth Regiment*, quotes Lieutenant Taggard, 471. Horace Porter is cited in Sommers, *Richmond Redeemed*, 77–78, and indicates that the shell went off. Lieutenant Taggard stated that it did not. This author has chosen to accept the eyewitness account of the lieutenant.

149. *OR*, vol. 42, part 2, Lincoln to Grant at 9:40 a.m., Grant to Lincoln, 1:40 p.m., 1090–91.

150. Ibid., Grant to Halleck, September 29, 1864, 10:45 a.m., 1091.

151. Ibid., Grant to Birney, September 29, 1864, 1114.

152. Sommers, *Richmond Redeemed*, 78.

153. Ripley, "First Hand Account." Butler had visited the New Market Heights front immediately preceding his brief visit to Chaffin's Farm.

154. *OR*, vol., 42, part 1, "Returns of Casualties in the "Union Forces", 134–36; Sommers, *Richmond Redeemed*, 483–84. Both the *OR* and

Sommers list Stannard's casualties as 760 and Heckman's as 513. In his report of April 18, 1865, Stannard wrote that his losses were 594, with none likely captured, on September 29.

CHAPTER 6

155. *OR*, vol. 42, part 2, Butler to Grant, 12:50 p.m., Grant to Butler, 1:35 p.m., 1110.

156. Laine and Penny, *Law's Alabama Brigade*, 302.

157. *OR*, vol. 42, part 2, Israel Sealy, Ass't Adjutant-General, to Butler, 1112; Sommers, *Richmond Redeemed*, 69–72.

158. Price, *Battle of New Market Heights*, 47–51. This work provides an excellent study of that battle.

159. Sommers, *Richmond Redeemed*, 78.

160. Manarin, *Henrico County*, 2:640–43.

161. Sommers, *Richmond Redeemed*, 80.

162. *OR*, vol. 42, part 1, Foster's Report of October 5, 1864, 760–61.

163. Jones, "Texas and Arkansas at Fort Harrison," 24.

164. Sommers, *Richmond Redeemed*, 83.

165. Manarin, *Henrico County*, 2:645.

166. Sommers, *Richmond Redeemed*, 84; *OR*, vol. 42, part 1, Foster's Report of October 5, 1864, 761.

167. Manarin, *Henrico County*, 2:646; *OR*, vol. 42, part 1, Foster's Report of October 5, 1864, 761.

168. Dr. Mowris of the 117th New York, cited in Manarin, *Henrico County*, 2:646.

169. Manarin, *Henrico County*, 2:647.

170. *O.R*, vol. 42, part 1, Foster's Report of October 5, 1864, 761.

171. *OR*, vol. 42, part 1, Report of Lieutenant Albert M. Barney, October 3, 1864, 765.

172. Silo, *115th New York*, 152–54. Quotes are from Lieutenant Nicholas De Graff.

173. Ibid., 154–56.

174. Jones, *Generals in Blue*, 24.

175. Mowris, *One Hundred and Seventeenth Regiment, N.Y. Volunteers*, 137–38.

176. Trudeau, *Like Men of War*, 296.

177. Manarin, *Henrico County*, 2:651; *OR*, vol. 41, part 1, "Return of Casualties in the Union Forces," 134.

178. *OR*, vol. 42, part 1, Report of Robert Foster, October 5, 1864, 760–61.

179. *OR*, vol. 42, part 2, Butler to Grant, 12:50 p.m. September 29, 1864, 1110; Sommers, *Richmond Redeemed*, 81.

180. Manarin, *Henrico County*, 652; Sommers, *Richmond Redeemed*, 88.

181. *OR*, vol. 42, part 1, Babcock's Report of October 1, 1864, 774–75.

182. *OR*, vol. 42, part 1, report of Major George E. Wagner to General Birney, October 6, 1864, 779–80; Manarin, *Henrico County*, 652–53, Sommers, *Richmond Redeemed*, 89.

183. *OR*, vol. 42, part 1, Colonel Shaw's report of October 9, 1864, 772.

184. Sommers, *Richmond Redeemed*, 90; Manarin, *Henrico County*, 2:653–54; *OR*, vol. 42, part 1, Report of James Shaw, October 9, 1864. For Captain Bailey's response, Manarin cites Califf, *Record of the Seventh Regiment U.S. Colored Troops*, 42.

185. *OR*, vol. 42, part 3, Letter from Captain Marcellus Bailey to Colonel James Shaw, October 16, 1864, 253.

186. Sommers, *Richmond Redeemed*, 90–91; Manarin, *Henrico County*, 2:654–55.

187. Charles Johnston letter to Jubal Early.

188. Lott, "Two Boys of the Fifth Texas Regiment," 416.

189. Trudeau, *Like Men of War*, 299.

190. John Purifoy Memoir, State of Alabama Archives.

191. Methvin, "My Military Services Rendered," 65; Details of the fight in the moat, with the rolling of the shells and the death of Corporal Dick, were repeated by veterans Perry in "Assault at Fort Gilmer," 415; Polley, *Hood's Texas Brigade*, 255–56; Judge Martin reports Captain J.R. Winder's letter, *Confederate Veteran* 13 (1905): 417; Granberry, "That Fort Gilmer Fight," 413.

192. "Points of Human Interest," *Richmond Whig*, October 6, 1864.

193. "Judge John H. Martin," *Confederate Veteran* 21 (1913).

194. Sommers, *Richmond Redeemed*, f.n.31, 517.

195. Manarin, *Henrico County*, 2:656–57; Lott, "Two Boys of the Fifth Texas Regiment," 417.

196. Sommers, *Richmond Redeemed*, 92.

197. *OR*, vol. 42, part 1, Return of Casualties in the Union Forces, 134, Report of Col. James Shaw, October 9, 1864, 773; Manarin, *Henrico County*, 2:658. Manarin states that the losses to the USCTs were 393.

198. Sommers, *Richmond Redeemed*, 92.

199. *OR*, vol. 42, part 2, Heckman's message to Butler, September 29, 1864, 1116.

200. Ibid., Ord's letter to Grant on September 29, 1115.

201. Sommers, *Richmond Redeemed*, 97–98; Manarin, *Henrico County*, 2:662.

202. *OR*, vol. 42, part 2, Grant to Butler, 1110.

203. Ibid., Butler to Grant, 1111.

204. Ripley quoted in Zeller, *Ninth Vermont*, 180.

205. Ripley, "First Hand Account."

206. *OR*, vol. 42, part 1, Stannard's Report of April 18, 1865, 800; Manarin, *Henrico County*, 2:677; Prescott, *Capture of Richmond*, 54; Sommers, *Richmond Redeemed*, 114.

207. The newly enclosed fort would be renamed "Fort Burnham," after the fallen Union general.

208. Benedict, *Vermont*, 2:247.

209. Ibid., 2:247–48.

210. Baker, "In Front of Richmond."

211. Ripley, "First Hand Account."

212. *OR*, vol. 42, part 1, Stannard's Report, 800.

213. Benedict, *Vermont in the Civil War*, 246.

214. Dr. Fairman quoted by Zeller, *Ninth Vermont*, 180.

215. John Purifoy's memoir.

Chapter 7

216. Porter Alexander, *Fighting for the Confederacy*, 477; *OR*, vol. 42, part 2, W.H. Taylor to Pickett, September 29, 1864, 1304; Taylor to Gregg, September 29, 1864, 1304–05; Ewell to General Bragg, September 29, 1864, 1303; Manarin, *Henrico County*, 2:678–79; Sommers, *Richmond Redeemed*, 116. McKethan had taken command of Clingman's Brigade after the latter had been wounded on August 19.

217. Pfanz, *Richard S. Ewell*, 417; Sommers, *Richmond Redeemed*, 95, 113; Manarin, *Henrico County*, 2:680.

218. Sommers, *Richmond Redeemed*, 114–15.

219. Ibid., 114–18; Manarin, *Henrico County*, 678.

220. *Richmond Whig*, September 30, 1864, cited in Manarin, *Henrico County*, 2:675.

221. *OR*, vol. 42, part 2, Butler to Grant, September 29, 1864, 9:10 p.m., 1111; Butler's General Order No. 116, 1146.

222. Ibid., Grant to General Meade, September 30, 1864, 8:15 a.m., 1118.

223. Ibid., Butler to Grant, September 30, 1864, 7:50 p.m., 1143–44.

224. Field, "Campaign of 1864 and 1865," 556.

225. Sommers, *Richmond Redeemed*, 126–32.

226. Ibid., 133–34.

227. Field, "Campaign of 1864 and 1865," 556–57.

228. Ibid., 557; Sommers, *Richmond Redeemed*, 137.

229. Manarin, *Henrico County*, 2:682; Sommers, *Richmond Redeemed*, 135–36.

230. Field, "Campaign of 1864 and 1865," 557; Sommers, *Richmond Redeemed*, 137–40.

231. *OR*, vol. 42, part 1, Ord's Report, April 18, 1865, 800.

232. Morgan, *Recollections of a Rebel Reefer*, 208.

233. Ripley, "First Hand Account."

234. Baker, "In Front of Richmond."

235. Thompson, *Thirteenth Regiment*, 481.

236. Bratton, "Operations of Bratton's Brigade."

237. *OR*, vol. 42, part 1, Report of James R. Hagood, December 20, 1864, 938.

238. Thompson, *Thirteenth Regiment*, 481.

239. Ripley, *Vermont General*, 251.

240. Kreutzer, *Notes and Observations*, 235.

241. Thompson, *Thirteenth Regiment*, 489.

242. Ibid., 486–87.

243. *OR*, vol. 42, part 1, Stannard's Report of April 18, 1865, 800–1.

244. Manarin, *Henrico County*, 2:684–88. Manarin cites Frank M. Mixson, *Reminisces of a Private: Company E, 1st S.C. Volunteers, Jenkins' Brigade, Lee's Army, 1861–1865* (Columbia, SC: State Company, 1910), 104.

245. Benedict, *Vermont*, 249.

246. Sommers, *Richmond Redeemed*, 141–42.

247. Ripley, *Vermont General*, 251; Humphreys, *Virginia Campaign*, 289; Zeller, *Ninth Vermont*, 182; Sommers, *Richmond Redeemed*, 143–44.

248. Sommers, *Richmond Redeemed*, 145; Freeman, *Lee's Lieutenants*, 3:593. Freeman mentioned several occasions that Hoke failed to fully cooperate in an attack. Among these were June 1 at Cold Harbor and the May 16 action at Drewry's Bluff.

249. Sommers, "Grant's Fifth Offensive," part 2, f.n.127, 532. A postwar account states that McKethan's men made it to the fort's barracks (Clark, *Regiments*, 3:214), Sommers cites correspondence from both McKethan and his inspector that most of the men did not make it that far and had to lie down in the "slight undulation" in the field.

250. Sommers, *Richmond Redeemed*, 145–46; Thompson, *Thirteenth Regiment*, 482; Clark, *Regiments*, 3:213; Prescott, *Capture of Richmond*.

251. Memoir from the William Henry von Eberstein Papers, East Carolina Manuscript Collection at the Joyner Library.

252. Burgwyn Papers, cited in Barefoot, *General Robert F. Hoke*, 225–26.

253. Clark, *Regiments*, 1:408, 4:497.

254. Sommers, *Richmond Redeemed*, 146–48.

255. Sommers, "Grant's Fifth Offensive," part 2, 507–8. Some accounts state that the Confederates sent three to four waves of attacks at the fort. Sommers's description does not mention this. What seems likely is the disjointed Confederate attacks might have seemed to participants as waves of attacks by units that had re-formed, when it is more probable that they were the separate attacks of Field's and Hoke's units.

256. Sommers, *Richmond Redeemed*, 147–48.

257. E. Porter Alexander Papers.

258. Moxley, *Recollections*, 252–53. Cited in Sommers, *Richmond Redeemed*, 156. Sommers questions the veracity of Sorrel's memory, stating that "wartime testimony from Alexander's headquarters indicates that Lee did intend to resume attacking on Saturday."

259. Manarin, *Henrico County,* 2:691.
260. Wallace, *American Heroism,* 519–20.
261. Sommers, *Richmond Redeemed,* 156–57.
262. Manarin, *Henrico County,* 2:693–94.

CHAPTER 8

263. Polley, *A Soldier's Letters,* 165.
264. Wright, "Bushrod Johnson's Men at Fort Harrison," 475.
265. *OR,* vol. 42, part 2, Butler to Ord, September 28, 1864, 1084–86.
266. *OR,* vol. 42, part 1, Ord's Report of June 15, 1865, 794.
267. Ripley, *Vermont General,* 252.
268. *Richmond Dispatch,* April 8, 1869.

CHAPTER 9

269. Manarin, *Henrico County,* 2:865.
270. Willett, *History of the RNBP,* 27.
271. Ibid., 29–30. Willett cites "Richmond Battlefield Parks acquired for the Public by Richmond Battlefield Parks Corporation." This is a pamphlet used to solicit contributions and is located in the Eckenrode Files, State Archives and Library, Richmond, Virginia.
272. Ibid., 30–34.
273. Ibid., 7.
274. Ibid., 35.
275. Ibid.
276. Ibid., 57–61.
277. Ibid., 71–72.

APPENDIX I

278. All Union entries are from Eicher and Eicher, *Civil War High Command;* Zeller, *Ninth Vermont,* 182.
279. Krick, *Lee's Colonels,* 46.
280. Jeffrey D. Wert, "Dudley McIver DuBose," *The Confederate Generals,* 2:78–79.
281. Donald C. Pfanz, "Richard Stoddert Ewell," *The Confederate Generals,* 2:111–12.
282. William C. Davis, "Charles William Field," *The Confederate Generals,* 2:124–25.
283. Ibid., "John Gregg," *The Confederate Generals,* 3:36–39.
284. Krick, *Staff Officers in Gray,* 282–83.

Bibliography

PRIMARY SOURCES

(RNBP = Richmond National Battlefield Park)
(SHSP = Southern Historical Society Papers, reprinted, Millwood, NY: Kraus Reprint Company.)

Alexander, Edward Porter. *Fighting for the Confederacy: The Personal Memoirs of General Edward Porter Alexander.* Edited by Gary W. Gallagher. Chapel Hill: University of North Carolina Press, 1989.

———. Papers. Southern Historical Collection. Wilson Library, University of North Carolina, Chapel Hill.

Alexander, J.M. "Army of the James: Fighting and Suffering Around Bermuda Hundred." *Nat'l Tribune,* July 31, 1890.

Allen, Cornelius T. "Fight at Chaffin's Farm, or Fort Harrison." *Confederate Veteran* 13 (1905).

Baker, H.E. "In Front of Richmond: Incidents on the Career of a Soldier During the Early Days of the Investment of the Rebel Capital." *Adirondack Record,* July 25, 1919.

Benedict, George G. *Vermont in the Civil War: A History of the Part Taken by the Vermont Soldiers and Sailors in the War for the Union 1861–5.* Vol. 2. Burlington, VT: Free Press Association, 1888.

Bratton, John. "Report on the Operations of Bratton's Brigade from May 7th, 1864 to January, 1865." *SHSP* 8 (1880).

Breckenridge, G.W. "Story of a Boy Captain." *Confederate Veteran* 13 (1905).

Burlington (VT) Free Press. "The Capture of Fort Harrison." January 20, 1865.

Butler, Benjamin F. *Butler's Book*. Boston: A.M. Thayer & Co., 1892.

————. *Private and Official Correspondence of Gen. Benjamin F. Butler During the Period of the Civil War*. Edited by Benjamin Franklin Butler and Jessie Ames Marshall. Privately issued, 1917.

Chamberlain, Joshua Lawrence. *The Passing of the Armies: An Account of the Final Campaign of the Army of the Potomac, Based Upon Personal Reminisces of the Fifth Army Corps*. New York: Barnes & Noble, 2004. Originally published in 1915.

Clay, Cecil. "Fort Harrison, How It Was Taken and the First Three Union Men on the Ramparts." *National Tribune*, March 22, 1888.

————. Letter to *Nat'l Tribune*. May 2, 1889.

————. Letter to *Weekly Times*. November 5, 1881.

Day, George L. "The Battle of Chaffin's Farm." *Richmond Times Dispatch*, October 4, 1936.

Delaware County Republican, October 14, 1864.

Depew, A.R. "The Capture of Fort Harrison." *National Tribune*, October 28, 1886.

Dowdey, Clifford, and Louis H. Manarin. *The Wartime Papers of R.E. Lee*. Boston: Little, Brown and Company, 1961.

Ellis, Henry J. Letter, October 2, 1864. Bell Wiley Collection, Emory University Special Collections.

Ewell, Richard S. "Memoranda of the Attack on the North Side James River 29th September 1864." Richard S. Ewell Letterbook.

Field, Major General C.W. "Campaign of 1864 and 1865." *SHSP* 14 (1886).

Flanigan, W.A. "That Fight at Fort Gilmer." *Confederate Veteran* 13 (1905).

Granberry, J.A.H. "That Fort Gilmer Fight." *Confederate Veteran* 13 (1905).

Grant, Ulysses S. *The Personal Memoirs of Ulysses S. Grant*. Old Saybrook, CT: Konecky & Konecky, 1886.

Hagood, J.R. *Southern Historical Society Papers* 13 (1885).

Henderson, E.M. "A Wounded Pennsylvanian." *Philadelphia Weekly Times*, April 21, 1883.

Hissong, James. Letter to *Nat'l Tribune*, July 21, 1887.

Humphreys, General Andrew A. *The Virginia Campaign, 1864 and 1865*. New York: DeCapo Press, 1995. Originally published 1883.

Hyde, William L. *History of the 112th N.Y.* Predonia, NY: McKinstry & Co., 1866.

Johnson, Charles. "Attack on Fort Gilmer, September 29, 1864." *Southern Historical Society Papers* 1 (1876).

————. Letter to General J.A. Early. N.d.

Johnston, J. Ambler. *Echoes of 1861–1961*. Privately printed, 2000.

Jones, A.C. "Texas and Arkansas at Fort Gilmer." *Confederate Veteran* 12 (1904).

Jones, John B. *A Rebel War Clerk's Diary*. Edited by Earl Schenck Miers. New York: Sagamore Press, Inc., 1958.

"Judge John H. Martin." *Confederate Veteran* 21 (1913).

Kreutzer, William. *Notes and Observations of the Ninety-Eighth N.Y. Volunteers in the War of 1861.* Philadelphia: Grant, Rodgers, 1878.

Lott, Jess B. "Two Boys of the Fifth Texas Regiment." *Confederate Veteran* 13 (1905).

Martin, John M. "The Assault Upon Fort Gilmer." *Confederate Veteran* 13 (1905).

———. "Forts Gilmer and Harrison Forces." *Confederate Veteran* 14 (1906).

———. "That Fort Gilmer Fight." *Confederate Veteran 13* (1905).

McGowan letter to *Houston Tri-Weekly Telegraph*, November 29, 1864.

Methvin, John Francis. "A Brief History of My Military Services Rendered." *Confederate Reminisces and Letters, 1861–1855.* Vol. 7. Atlanta: Georgia Division, UDC, 1998.

Moore, James B. "The Attack of Fort Harrison." *Confederate Veteran* 13 (1905).

Moore, Thomas. "Memories of a Civil War Veteran." *Sandy Creek News*, February 26, 1953.

Morgan, James Morris. *Recollections of a Rebel Reefer.* Boston: Houghton Mifflin Company, 1917.

Mowris, J.A. *A History of the One Hundred and Seventeenth Regiment, N.Y. Volunteers.* Hamilton, NY: Edmonston Publishing, 1996. Originally published Hartford, CT: Case, Lockwood and Co., 1866.

Neel, W.S. "One of 'Old Rock's Brigade." *Atlanta Journal*, April 19, 1902.

New York Times. "The Fight at Chapin's Farm." October 2, 1864.

Oliver, L.C. "New Hampshire at Fort Harrison." *National Tribune*, January 13, 1887.

Paine, Charles J. Letters. RNBP.

Perry, Herman H. "The Assault at Fort Gilmer." *Confederate Veteran* 13 (1905).

Pickens, J.D. "Fort Harrison." *Confederate Veteran* 21 (October 1913).

Polley, Joseph B. *Hood's Texas Brigade.* Dayton, OH: Morningside Bookshop, 1988.

———. "Polley Lost a Foot—A Furlough." *Confederate Veteran* 5 (September 1897).

———. *A Soldier's Letters to Charming Nellie.* Edited by Richard B. McCaslin, Knoxville: University of Tennessee Press, 2008. Originally printed 1908.

Prescott, R.B. *The Capture of Richmond.* The Siege of Petersburg Online, Military Order of the Loyal Legion of the United States. Used by permission. http://www.beyondthecrater.com/resources/mollus/massachusetts-mollus/mollus-ma-the-capture-of-richmond.

Purifoy, John. Memoir. State of Alabama Archives.

Report of Christopher J. Tubbs, Headquarters, Fifty-eighth Pennsylvania Volunteers. October 2, 1864.

Richmond Daily Enquirer. "A Letter to the Editor." Signed "Howitzer." October 20, 1864.

Richmond Sentinel. "Letter Concerning the Battle of Fort Harrison." October 12, 1864.

Richmond Whig, October 6, 1864.

Ripley, Edward Hastings. "Gives First Hand Account of Battle of Fort Harrison." *Richmond News Leader*, April 27, 1939.

———. *Vermont General: The Letters of Edward Hastings Ripley*. Edited by Sybil Huntington Ripley. New York: Devin-Adair Company, 1960.

Rock, R.S. "War Reminisces." *Confederate Veteran* 9 (1901).

Smith, M.V. "Fort Harrison." *Confederate Veteran* 21 (1913).

Sorrel, G. Moxley. *Recollections of a Confederate Staff Officer*. Edited by Bell Irvin Wiley. Wilmington, NC: Broadfoot Publishing Company, 1991.

Taylor, R.C. "Personal Experience of Major Richard C. Taylor." Unpublished. Cited in Calrow. RNBP.

Taylor, Walter Heron. *Lee's Adjutant: The Wartime Letters of Colonel Walter Herron Taylor, 1862–1865*. Edited by R. Lockwood Tower. Columbia: University of South Carolina Press, 1995.

Thompson, S. Millett. *History of the Thirteenth Regiment of New Hampshire Volunteer Infantry in the War of the Rebellion 1861–1865*. Boston: Houghton, Mifflin and Company, 1888.

U.S. War Department. *The War of the Rebellion: A Compilation of the Official Records of the Union and Confederate Armies, Vol. 42, Series 1, Parts I, II, III*. Washington, D.C: U.S. Government Printing Office, 1893.

Van Lew, Elizabeth. Papers. Special Collection, Swem Library, College of William and Mary.

———. *A Yankee Spy in Richmond: The Civil War Diary of "Crazy Bet" Van Lew*. Edited by David D. Ryan. Mechanicsburg, PA: Stackpole Books, 1996.

Von Eberstein, William Henry. Papers. East Carolina Manuscript Collection. J.Y. Joyner Library, East Carolina University, Greenville, North Carolina.

Waite, Major Otis F.R. *New Hampshire in the Great Rebellion*. Claremont, NH: Tracy, Chase & Co., 1870.

Wallace, Lew. *The Story of American Heroism: Thrilling Narratives of Personal Adventures During the Great Civil War, as Told by the Medal Winners and Roll of Honor Men*. Springfield, OH: J.W. Jones, 1897.

Ware, E. "Battery Harrison: A Graphic Sketch by a Comrade of the 13th New Hampshire." *National Tribune*, January 20, 1887.

White, William S. "A Diary of the War, or What I Saw of It." From *Contributions to a History of the Richmond Howitzer Battalion*. Baltimore, MD: Butternut and Blue, 2000.

Wickman, Donald H., ed. *Letters to Vermont, From Her Civil War Soldier Correspondents to the Home Press*. Vol 2. Bennington, VT: Images from the Past, 1998.

Wright, Marcus J. "Bushrod Johnson's Men at Fort Harrison." *Confederate Veteran* 14 (December 1906).

SECONDARY SOURCES

Barefoot, Daniel W. *General Robert F. Hoke: Lee's Modest Warrior*. Winston-Salem, NC: John F. Blair, Publisher, 1996.

"Battle of Fort Harrison or Chaffin's Farm—September 29–30, 1864." Unpublished document in files at RNBP. No name or date.

Beyer, W.F., and O.F. Keydel. *Deeds of Valor: How America's Civil War Heroes Won the Congressional Medal of Honor.* Stamford, CT: Long Meadow Press, 1903.

Calcutt, Rebecca Barbour. *Richmond's Wartime Hospitals.* Gretna, LA: Pelican Publishing, 2005.

Calrow, Charles J. "Battle of Chaffin's Farm: Fort Harrison: A Study." Unpublished, RNBP files, 1932.

Catton, Bruce. *The Army of the Potomac: Mr. Lincoln's Army.* New York: Doubleday & Company, 1951.

Clark, Walter, ed. *Histories of the Several Regiments and Battalions From North Carolina in the Great War 1861–'65.* Raleigh, NC: E.M. Uzzell, 1901. Reprint, Wendell, NC: Broadfoot Publishing, 1982.

Claxton, Melvin, and Mark Puls. *Uncommon Valor: A Story of Race, Patriotism and Glory in the Final Battles of the Civil War.* Hoboken, NJ: John Wiley & Sons, Inc., 2006.

Cornish, Dudley Taylor. *The Sable Arm: Negro Troops in the Union Army, 1861–1865.* New York: W.W. Norton Company, 1966. Originally published 1956.

Coski, John M. *Capital Navy: The Men, Ships and Operations of the James River Squadron.* New York: Savas-Beatie, 1996. Reprint, 2005.

Damerel, John E. "1864 in 1983: A Tour of the Roads Used in the Movement Against Richmond in the Fort Harrison Sector, September 29, 1864." Unpublished, 1983. RNBP.

Davis, William C. *Death in the Trenches.* Alexandria, VA: Time-Life Books, 1986.

Davis, William C., and Julia Hoffman, eds. *The Confederate Generals.* 4 vols. National Historical Society, 1991.

Dickinson, Clifford. *Union and Confederate Engineering Operations at Chaffin's Bluff/Chaffin's Farm, June 1862–April 3, 1865.* RNBP, 1989.

Dickson, Christopher. "Second Vermont Biographies/Obituaries." vermontcivilwar.org/units/2bgd/obits.php?input=5603.

Dowdey, Clifford. *Lee's Last Campaign: The Story of Lee and His Men Against Grant—1864.* New York: Skyhorse Publishing, 2011. Originally published 1960.

———. *The Seven Days: The Emergence of Robert E. Lee.* New York: Fairfax Press, 1964.

Driver, Robert J., Jr. *Richmond Local Defense Troops, C.S.A.* Wilmington, NC: Broadfoot Publishing Company, 2011.

Eggleston, Larry G. *Women in the Civil War.* Jefferson, NC: McFarland & Company, 2003.

Eicher, David J., and John H. Eicher. *Civil War High Command.* Stanford, CA: Stanford University Press, 2001.

Freeman, Douglas Southall. *Lee's Lieutenants: A Study in Command.* New York: Charles Scribner's Sons, 1942.

———. *R.E. Lee: A Biography.* New York: Charles Scribner's Sons, 1934.

Fuller, Colonel J.F.C. *The Generalship of Ulysses S. Grant.* New York: Dodd, Meade & Company, 1929.

Gallagher, Gary W. *Lee the Soldier.* Lincoln: University of Nebraska Press, 1996.

Glathaar, Joseph T. *General Lee's Army: From Victory to Collapse.* New York: Free Press, 2008.

Hardaway, Colonel Robert A. Letter.

Johnston, J. Ambler. *Echoes of 1861–1961.* Richmond, VA: Privately printed, 2000.

———. *To Various People Who May Be Interested in Why the Name "Fort Harrison."* RNBP files.

Jones, Wilmer L. *Generals in Blue and Gray.* Mechanicsburg, PA: Stackpole Books, 2006. Originally published 2004.

Krick, R.E.L. *Staff Officers in Gray: A Biographical Register of the Staff Officers in the Army of Northern Virginia.* Chapel Hill: University of North Carolina Press, 2003.

Krick, Robert K. *Lee's Colonels.* 5th ed. Wilmington, NC: Broadfoot Publishing, 2009.

Laine, J. Gary, and Morris M. Penny. *Law's Alabama Brigade in the War Between the Union and the Confederacy.* Shippensburg, PA: White Maine Publishing, 1996.

Manarin, Louis H. *Henrico County Field of Honor.* Vol. 2. Henrico County, VA. Published by Henrico County, 2004.

McMurray, Richard M. *Virginia Military Institute Alumni in the Civil War.* Lynchburg, VA: H.E. Howard, 1999.

McPherson, James M. *Battle Cry of Freedom: The Civil War Era.* New York: Oxford University Press, 1988.

———. *Tried by War: Abraham Lincoln as Commander in Chief.* New York: Penguin Press, 2008.

Nance, Leslie. "Fort Harrison." Unpublished, RNBP.

Nosworthy, Brent. *The Bloody Crucible of Courage.* New York: Carroll & Gray, 2003.

Paradis, James M. *Strike the Blow for Freedom: The 6th United States Colored Infantry in the Civil War.* Shippensburg, PA: White Maine Books, 1998.

Pfanz, Donald C. *Richard. S. Ewell: A Soldier's Life.* Chapel Hill: University of North Carolina Press, 1998.

Potter County Historical Society Quarterly Bulletin, July 2006.

Price, James S. *The Battle of New Market Heights: Freedom Will Be Theirs by the Sword.* Charleston, SC: The History Press, 2011.

Robertson, William Glenn. *Back Door to Richmond: The Bermuda Hundred Campaign, April–June 1864.* Baton Rouge: Louisiana State University Press, 1987.

Rhea, Gordon C. *The Battle for Spotsylvania Court House and the Road to Yellow Tavern, May 7–12, 1864.* Baton Rouge: Louisiana State University Press, 1997.

———. *The Battle of the Wilderness.* Baton Rouge: Louisiana State University Press, 1994.

———. *Cold Harbor: Grant and Lee May 26–June 3, 1864.* Baton Rouge: Louisiana State University Press, 2002.

Rhodes, Steven B., and Christopher Harte. "Fort Harrison." Unpublished, December 1979, RNBP.

Shadman, George, Jr. *They Marched on Richmond: The Story of the 148th New York Volunteers.* Watkins Glen, NY: Shaman, 1994.

Silo, Mark. *The 115th New York in the Civil War.* Jefferson, NC: McFarland & Company, 2007.

Simpson, Colonel Harold B. *Hood's Texas Brigade: Lee's Grenadier Guard.* Waco, TX: Texian Press, 1970.

Smith, John David, ed. *Black Soldiers in Blue: African American Troops on the Civil War Era.* Chapel Hill: University of North Carolina Press, 2002.

Sommers, Richard J. "Fury at Fort Harrison." *Civil War Times Illustrated*, October 1980.

———. "Grant's Fifth Offensive at Petersburg: A Study in Strategy, Tactics and Generalship." PhD diss., Rice University, 1970.

———. *Richmond Redeemed: The Siege at Petersburg.* Garden City, NY: Doubleday & Company, Inc. 1981.

Suderow, Bryce. "First Deep Bottom and the Crater." Unpublished.

———. "Grant's and Meade's Learning Curves." Unpublished.

———. "Second Deep Bottom, Globe Tavern, and Reams Station." Unpublished.

Trudeau, Noah Andre. *The Last Citadel: Petersburg, Virginia June 1864–April, 1865.* Baton Rouge: Louisiana State University Press, 1991.

———. *Like Men of War: Black Troops in the Civil War 1862–1865.* New York: Little, Brown and Company, 1998.

Warner, Ezra J. *Generals in Blue: Lives of the Union Commanders.* Baton Rouge: Louisiana State University Press, 1964.

Wickman, Don. *We Are Coming Father Abraham: The History of the 9th Vermont Volunteer Infantry, 1862–1865.* Lynchburg, VA: Schroeder Publications, 2005.

Willett, John T. "A History of the Richmond National Battlefield Park." Manuscript at RNBP, 1957.

Williams, Edward B. *Hood's Texas Brigade in the Civil War.* Jefferson, NC: McFarland & Company, 2012.

Zeller, Paul G. *The Ninth Vermont Infantry: A History and Roster.* Jefferson, NC: McFarland & Company, Inc., 2008.

Index

About the Author

D oug Crenshaw is a strategic IT sourcing manager who has studied history at Randolph Macon College and the University of Richmond. A volunteer for the Richmond National Battlefield Park, Crenshaw is an avid history enthusiast and member of the Richmond Civil War Roundtable.

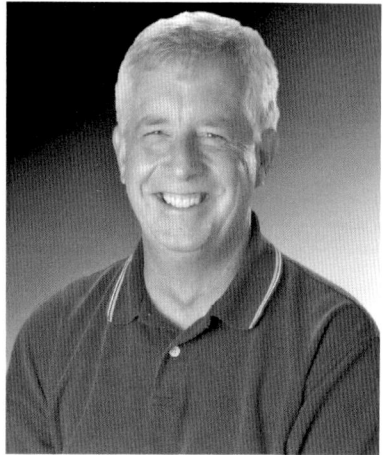